ALOHA

- MADE WITH LOVE -

- X X X X -

Mutual Love

"Hollan is an amazing person, and her love-infused vegan food is incredible. I would fly thousands of miles to Hawaii to enjoy any one her many delicious meals. With her beautiful book Good Food Gratitude, I can prepare and devour these creative and tasty recipes at home without hopping on an airplane, and now so can you. Mahalo Hollan!"

Lewis Howes, founder of *The School of Greatness* and bestselling New York Times author of *The Mask of Masculinity* and *The School of Greatness*

"Chef Hollan brings a refreshing island twist with Good Food Gratitude and her delicious plant-based recipes. Her thoughtful perspective on food, her engaging story, and her captivating photos make you feel like you are experiencing this awesome health journey with her!"

Alkemiah Earth, holistic lifestyle coach, energetic healer

"In Good Food Gratitude, Hollan has created a vegan cookbook with a wide range of delicious recipes presented with gorgeous imagery. Whether a novice cook or an expert in the kitchen, these homestyle dishes are sure to become your go-to favorites."

Marie Oser, bestselling author and executive producer, VegTV

"Since I met Hollan some of my best memories are going to her house and eating delicious home-cooked plant-based food. Her fantastic recipe book Good Food Gratitude definitely brought back those memories and now I'm able to cook those wonderful recipes at home! Good Food Gratitude really embraces the Aloha spirit thru these amazing recipes."

Brianna Cope, pro surfer

"Good Food Gratitude offers easy delicious nourishing family friendly food that celebrates a vegan lifestyle with tropical flair and stunning photographs."

Brigitte Mars, author of *The Country Almanac of Home Remedies* and *Natural First Aid*

"Hollan's gorgeous book, Good Food Gratitude, is as inviting as she is and clearly created through her love. This book will reignite one's passion for cooking through her delicious recipes. Her words have always empowered me to live my healthiest life and now you can experience her magic through easy and sustainable lifestyle hacks. A must have."

Dr. Jen Esquer, PT, DPT, founder of The Mobility Method and The Optimal Body

"I opened Hollan's beautiful cookbook Good Food Gratitude—and found I'd flown to heaven! Or maybe Hawaii, where all the foods that Hollan guides us to create are delectable, colorful and too sinfully luscious to be healthy. Except that every recipe in her book is actually healthy even if called "pizza," "pancakes," or "lasagna." I've only gratitude and admiration for how Hollan's culinary works of art will change my life easily and happily."

Cyndi Dale, author of 25 bestselling spiritual books including *The Subtle Body* series

**EASY TO PREPARE VEGAN
HOME-STYLE RECIPES
+ BEACH INSPIRED LIFESTYLE TIPS
FOR THE ENTIRE FAMILY**

GOOD FOOD
Gratitude
HOLLAN HAWAII

DEEPER WELL
PUBLISHING

Published by: Deeper Well Publishing, deeperwellpublishing.com
Creative Director: Anthony J.W. Benson, injoiCreative.com
Book designed by: Gayna Murphy, CharLee Christian, and Anthony J.W. Benson
Edited by: Peggy Paul Casella

Printed in the United States of America

ISBN: 978-0-9857152-7-4

Library of Congress Control Number: 2018966157

For press inquiries, email: publicity@deeperwellpublishing.com

Photographers:
Alana Blanchard - 9
Blenda Montoro Miller - cover, 12, 16, 51, 66, 83, 95, 105, 106, 141, 216, 251, 252
Heather Ransley - 2, 13
Grubfather - 16
Bryce Johnson - 24, 25, 35, 36, 52, 65, 69, 73, 84, 111, 128, 153, 173, 174, 177, 206, 209, 210, 214
Haleem Hamid - 26, 27, 251
Elliot Lucas - 39, 40, 43, 44, 47, 48, 55, 56, 59, 60, 70, 74, 77, 79, 80, 89, 91, 92, 96, 99, 100, 108,
115, 116, 119, 123, 125, 131, 142, 145, 148, 154, 157, 158, 161, 162, 165, 166, 169, 178, 184,
193-94, 205, 213, 217, 218, 219, 220, 222, 223, 226, 232, 233, 237, 238, 241, 242, 243, 244
Kilikai Ahuna - 112, 132, 138, 147
Tom Locke - 127, 182, 184, 185, 240

Additional images used under licenses by Shutterstock, 123RF, iStock and Depositphotos.

DISCLAIMER: The recipes, ideas, concepts, and opinions expressed in *Good Food Gratitude* are
intended to help readers make thoughtful and informed decisions about their diet and health.
This book is sold with the understanding that author and publisher are not rendering medical or
nutritional advice of any kind, nor is this book intended to replace medical or nutritional advice,
nor to diagnose, prescribe, or treat any disease, condition, illness, or injury. It should not be
used as a substitute for treatment by or the advice of a professional health care provider. It is
recommended that you receive full medical clearance from a licensed health care provider before
beginning any diet or health program, including any aspect of *Good Food Gratitude*. Although the
author and publisher have endeavored to ensure that the information provided herein is complete
and accurate, the author and publisher claim no responsibility to any person or entity for any
liability, loss, or damage caused or alleged to be caused directly or indirectly as a result of the use,
application, or interpretation of the material in this book or any errors or omissions herein.
The Food and Drug Administration has not evaluated the statements contained in this book,
Good Food Gratitude.

TO MY CHILDREN,
AND ONE DAY
THEIR CHILDREN

MADE WITH LOVE
- X X X X -

Foreword

Seven years ago, I went full vegan. I had been raised vegetarian, so it wasn't the hardest switch to make, not as big a leap as it is for some people. But I had started to notice that I just didn't feel that good when I ate dairy. And I noticed that I did feel good when I ate a lot of fruits and veggies and other plant foods instead. So I started thinking about making the switch.

The idea of going completely vegan was a little scary at first because there was so much out there saying that you can't get proper nutrition if you're a vegan—especially that you can never get enough protein. But I wondered how much of that was true, and I decided to do my own research. I learned that not only was there a lot of misinformation flying around, but some of it was coming from people who had a financial interest in keeping everybody's diet just the way it was. I learned that you can do just fine eating only plants, get all the protein you need, and feel even better than before, without anything in your diet. That definitely turned out to be true for me. I'm a professional athlete, and I surf all over the world. And believe me, I get plenty of power from eating vegan and I don't miss dairy at all.

I met Hollan when I bumped into her one day on Kauai, the island where we both live and where she had her restaurant Caffe Coco. By the time we met, I had been vegan for a while, and I was interested in learning how to get better at cooking vegan so I could show friends and family what amazing food you can have. Hollan offered to teach me a few things in the kitchen at her restaurant, and in between my travels, I took her up on that offer several times.

Hollan is such a bubbly person, and a brilliant chef and teacher, and when you walked into her restaurant you felt welcome right away. If you didn't already know it going in, you couldn't even tell it was a vegan place just by looking around—you just saw and smelled all kinds of good food that looked beautiful on the plate. Hollan's dishes are all really healthy, like you'd expect, but they're also so delicious! I love all her savory things: her sandwiches, and her creative way with appetizers. And then there are the "naughty" foods—her brownies and cookies are amazing! The recipes for those, as well as dozens of other amazing dishes, are here in this book. I've made her sweet treats for my friends, and they had no idea they were vegan, let alone healthier—they just knew they were delicious, and those treats disappeared fast.

What you eat is going to determine how you feel, and if you want to feel your best you should eat only the best foods nature has to offer. Hollan knows how to prepare those foods in ways that taste great, satisfy just about everybody, and make you feel fantastic. I've learned a lot from Hollan, and now, with *Good Food Gratitude*, you can too!

Alana Blanchard

Pro Surfer and Mom

ALOHA

Hello there

HOLLAN
HAWAII

HOLLAN IS A VEGAN CHEF, MOM, HEALTH ADVOCATE AND AUTHOR.

KAUAI

when you begin to listen, your body
will communicate its needs on a level you
might not have known even existed.

If you look at my life through my Instagram, you might think I have it all, living the life of my dreams—a beautiful family, passion and purpose, all on the tranquil island of Kauai. Good Food Gratitude is a culmination of my journey toward healthfulness. In these pages, I share with you everything I have researched, tried, learned, embraced, and adopted along the way.

The book in your hands represents all that is me and what I value most in my life: My home in Kauai, healthy food, living sustainably, travel, family, and friends. Sharing gives me room to continue to grow by making space for new experiences. I have realized over time what health really means to me. It means listening to my body's ever-changing needs and always fulfilling those needs. It is a continuous journey that I cannot blink an eye to. I encourage you to really listen to what your body is asking of you—not just in this moment, but every day. I promise you one thing: when you begin to listen, your body will communicate its needs on a level you might not have known even existed.

Food has become the centerpiece of my life. It all started for me when I first went to culinary school at Le Cordon Bleu in San Francisco in 2000. At that point, learning about food was simply for pure enjoyment and education. When I became vegan after reading the book *Skinny Bitch*, I found so many benefits physically and mentally that there was no going back. Health food truly became my universe and is the north star navigating my life. I see it as a full-time job to keep my family and myself nourished, educated, and in balance—with healthy, nourishing, plant-based foods. Over the years, I have learned to foster my body according to its daily needs rather than a set routine. I make recipes to support my active lifestyle, to lower my stress level, or to increase my energy . . . depending on the day and my body's requirements.

Find what works for you by listening to your body. Discover what foods make you feel alive and energized. Recognize what foods make you feel irritable or sluggish. This will enhance the relationship between yourself and your overall well-being, and perhaps even prolong your life. I believe that we should know our bodies better than anyone, even our doctors. This is something that no one told me as a child. It has taken me a long time to discover that I have the capability to know my body on such a level—all I had to do is learn how to listen. I don't hold the only keys to health, but I do have a keychain of experiences that I want to share. In doing so, I hope to assist in the process of incorporating health, self-love, and wellness into people's lives. Everyone is unique, so finding what works for each of us by really getting to know our own bodies is a vast, exciting challenge, as well as an immense life-changer. Start by discovering what works for you.

During my free time, which I always make sure to create, I search for waterfalls, swim in the ocean with turtles, lie under the shade of a palm tree on a dreamy beach, climb the most beautiful mountains for mind-blowing views—either by myself when alone time is needed, or with my family and friends.

On a normal work day, you may find me in the kitchen cooking, filming videos, writing blog posts, catering for celebrities on their private jets or in their homes, and developing recipes—sometimes all in the same day! My personal and business travels push me to step outside the norms of everyday life and allow me to focus on what I love: learning new recipes, exploring flavors, and experiencing other people's ideas on health, wellness, food, and cooking.

On a normal work day, you may find me in the kitchen cooking, filming videos, writing blog posts, catering for celebrities on their private jets or in their homes, and developing recipes—sometimes all in the same day!

The most fulfilling part of my travels has been learning from others. I have spent time in Los Angeles and New York, learning and eating from many different chefs at many different restaurants. Last year, I realized my dream of traveling internationally with the purpose of learning cooking techniques from different cultures. Cuba was my first trip. I was amazed by how they cook and what ingredients they cook with. Recently, I traveled to Europe and Greece and learned about so many cuisines. In the book, I share some tips and skills that I have adapted to my cooking.

I also enjoy deconstructing and recreating my favorite dishes. I want to show people that you can have your favorite foods, but healthier! In doing so, you may see expansive changes in your body, mood, and consciousness.

It makes perfect sense that my life centers around food on this magical island, floating in the middle of the Pacific. I am so excited to introduce myself to you, give you a glimpse of my life, and share my deep love for food in this cookbook.

Enjoy!

MADE WITH LOVE
X X X X

Recently I traveled to Rome, Paris, London, and Greece. I will share everything I learned and the way I am adapting my new skills and tricks into my cooking.

MADE WITH LOVE

- X X X X -

About Me

I grew up in the San Francisco Bay Area and always loved the variety of food all around me. Since I was one of six kids, meals at my house were about feeding the masses as easily as possible—quantity over quality. However, my mom would make me a veggie version of whatever she had cooking, encouraging my vegetarianism from the start.

My grandmother always entertained in style. She was proper and all about etiquette. When I was a kid, she put me in manners classes, where I learned all about dining with respect and style. I find my approach to life and food now is somewhere in between my mother and grandmother. As a teenager, I added meat to my diet, and I started to have a lot of negative symptoms and health issues. At the time, I did not associate these problems with meat or dairy. Looking back, it is hard to ignore that the more meat and dairy I ate, the more problems I had. I always loved food, but it wasn't until I started traveling in my teen years that I realized how special the food in San Francisco really was and still is.

During my brief modeling career, I used food to keep my body at a certain weight (it was during the unhealthy waif craze), and my relationship with food became blurred. Did I eat to live or live to eat? It would change from day to day, and many times I ate to be thin. My love affair

with food was an on again–off again fling. At 21, after having a six-week-long love affair with all foods, I realized I was pregnant. I then used pregnancy as an excuse to throw all food rules out the kitchen window. I couldn't believe how good food could taste. After I had my first child, I tried to be the perfect stay-at-home mom and wife by preparing a three-course meal every night. I had so much fun in the kitchen planning meals, cooking, and entertaining. I enjoyed it so much, I decided to put myself through culinary school, specializing in pastries at Le Cordon Bleu in San Francisco. After graduating and having my second child, I could only work restaurant jobs with more pay and shorter hours, which were always in the front of the house, not the kitchen. I worked in hotels and dining for about ten years. During this time, I became slightly obsessed with food and catering. I fulfilled my passion for food by working in catering, event planning, serving, and restaurant/hotel management. With unrelenting dreams of palm trees and beaches, we eventually packed up the family and made the move across the Pacific to Hawaii.

After my third child was born, I began searching for better health, and I read *Skinny Bitch*, a book on veganism that changed my life completely. I read everything I could get my hands on to

19

better understand food choices and health. I learned about new and exciting ingredients and recipes that reignited my love for cooking. In order to eat a vegan diet that actually tasted good, I had to channel my culinary skills to create scrumptious, nutritious vegan recipes of my own.

One day, my husband and I were driving down a local road in Kauai, and we saw a cute café with a "for sale" sign on it. On a whim, we decided to use our savings and buy it. The restaurant has given me the time to perfect my craft, which is home-style vegan cooking. All of the recipes in this book have been tested not only by my family and friends, but by the thousands of customers we serve from around the world. At the end of 2017, after six and a half years of love, sweat, and tears, I sold the café so I could complete this book, write more books, create videos, and teach what I have learned along the way.

I believe that health is not only about food—it is about finding and doing what makes you happy, and adopting a lifestyle choice that supports you in wellness. With that being said, I am dedicated to practicing what I preach. People always tell me that if they had someone like me in their daily life, then they could be vegan. This book is my attempt to help you do just that. These recipes are here to inspire you about this lifestyle and to nourish you, your family, and our planet.

For the love of Vegan

Veganism is not just a diet—it is the conscious decision not to eat or purchase products that come from an animal. All of the yummy recipes here are free of fish, meat, poultry, eggs, and dairy (yes, butter and cheese, too!). I dare you to try to find something missing from the taste and nutrition of these thoughtfully crafted dishes.

When I started exploring how to be healthier, I tried many different food regimens and eating habits. Veganism was the one style of eating that made me feel my best, and that I never felt like quitting. Ten years ago, I started working and reworking recipes to transform non-vegan dishes into vegan dishes—a true passion of mine!

My goal was to always create an herbivorous harmony of taste and health. The recipes in this book range from super healthy to a little bit less healthy—everything in moderation, right? But, they are all healthier versions of the original recipes you may already know. Go ahead and give them a try! They are all easy to prepare and delicious to eat, and they will make your body sing, "Thank you!" Although it started with my health, I find that not eating animals also matches my consciousness. It doesn't take more than a couple Google searches to see that animals are being exploited for meat and milk. I feel better knowing that I am not contributing to this. A plant-based vegan lifestyle is a way to walk a gentler path for animals and the planet. May this book guide you to a healthier, happier life for all living beings—especially for you and your family.

Gluten Free... is it for me?

Gluten is a protein found in wheat, barley, rye, spelt, and other cereal grains, that can be difficult to digest for some people.

I have found that sometimes my body reacts to wheat or gluten, and other times it doesn't. This has led me to develop a love/hate relationship with grains, as I never know how they will affect me. So, for the most part, I try to only eat gluten in moderation. If I feel it is not working for me, I give my system a chance to recover by not eating it at all.

Interestingly, I have found that when I eat gluten-free grains in abundance, I start to have the same issues as if I were eating glutenous foods. Over the years, I have attributed this to what I call the abundance factor: when I eat an abundance of processed foods (breads, crackers, chips,

cookies), my body doesn't handle it well and starts giving me cues (disease and symptoms), and I adjust where I can.

Many people have a disease related to gluten called celiac disease. For those with celiac disease, even a pinch of gluten is extremely toxic to their system, blocking the body's ability to process nutrients and resulting in an abundance of digestive issues. If you suspect gluten is wreaking havoc on your system, there is an easy test you can perform: stop eating it and see how you feel. Once again, it's about listening to your body. I've labeled all the gluten-free recipes in this book. For some of the recipes that aren't gluten free, I provide ideas on how to convert them if you are avoiding gluten.

Eat for the Planet!

I think we can all agree that our world is plagued by many conundrums. This book is my small contribution to guide you to live a more empowered life while also supporting our planet. I truly believe our biggest voice in this world is how we spend our hard-earned money. I choose to give my dollars to businesses and farmers that practice consciousness and sustainability while providing us with quality products. I buy all my ingredients 100-percent organic, and therefore I don't worry about GMOs (genetically modified organisms). I constantly research companies to make sure they are practicing what they preach. All of this takes a little time, but it's the little things like this that can make a big difference for our food quality, our health, and our planet. In the back of the book, you will find ideas I have for lessening your footprint when entertaining, eating, and being a consumer.

This cookbook is really a dream come true. You buying *Good Food Gratitude* is an even bigger dream come true—it means I am reaching people who are curious and like-minded beyond the confines of my kitchen. Also, together we are creating a community where we can support and learn from each other to live our healthiest lives and feel vital and worthy. Please reach out to me via email, Instagram, Twitter, YouTube, Facebook, or my website (HollanHawaii.com), and subscribe to my newsletter. Let's keep this conversation going!

GOOD

FOOD

GRATITUDE

MADE WITH LOVE
♥
X X X X

MADE WITH LOVE
x x x x

EVERY ONE
OF MY RECIPES
STARTS WITH
TWO THINGS

1.

LOVE

ALL MY RECIPES ARE ALWAYS MADE WITH ORGANIC INGREDIENTS AND I PREFER TO USE EXTRA VIRGIN OLIVE OIL.

MADE WITH LOVE
- - X X X X - -

2.
ORGANIC
FOOD

LEADING RESEARCH SHOWS THAT
LOVE + ORGANIC FOOD ARE BETTER
FOR YOUR HEALTH THAN ANYTHING

JUICES
MILKS
SMOOTHIES

Make your own

HOW TO MAKE
ANY SEED
or Nut Milk

PREP + COOK TIME 5 MINUTES **SERVES** 1 QUART

1 cup organic raw almonds

7 cups water

2 tablespoons maple syrup
(optional)

In a blender, mix the almonds with the water, gradually taking it to high speed. When the almonds are completely pulverized, strain the mixture through a nut milk bag into a large bowl. Add maple syrup and stir. Transfer the milk to a pitcher and store it in the fridge, covered, for up to 4 days.

Recipe Notes:

- You can use any nut or seed in place of the almonds. For example I love to make macadamia nut–coconut milk for açai bowls and smoothies. I have tried and love cashews, sesame seeds, and coconut. They all are tasty in their own way, and some go better with different recipes. Have fun, and find the one that makes your taste buds happy.

- I use a nut milk bag to strain my nut milk. You can find nut milk bags for sale at almost all health food stores. If you cannot find one, a paint strainer from a hardware store will work, or you can just use a clean dish towel or cheese cloth to strain it.

- There are many things you can do with the leftover pulp; however, these days I compost it.

- Almonds are naturally alkalizing, as is this recipe. Almonds are rich in protein, fiber, vitamins, antioxidants, and flavonoids. Almonds contain lots of healthy fats, magnesium, and vitamin E.

X GF

X SF

X NF (IF YOU USE HEMP,
COCONUT, OR SEED MILK

Making your own non-dairy milk is as simple as blending nuts or seeds with water, then straining. I like adding in a little maple syrup for sweetness. Almond milk is my go-to, and I use it for pretty much anything that calls for milk. I find it versatile, my body loves it, and my recipes come out great. You can change the recipe to suit your taste buds—more almonds, more maple syrup, more water—but this is how I like it. You can always buy nut milk in stores, but making your own is special because you have complete control over the ingredients.

This refreshing smoothie is like a juice—but with no juicing required. You will be getting all the nutrition and fiber, because I don't remove the pulp like a juicer does. I love that this smoothie is 100-percent Hawaiian. When you make it at home, let it transport you back to the beach.

ON A BEACH IN HAWAII SMOOTHIE

Local Green Dream

PREP + COOK TIME 5 MINUTES **MAKES** (16-OUNCE) SERVING

1 cup chopped kale leaves
   (I prefer curly kale)
½ cup chopped cucumber
1½ cups frozen chopped mango
1 cup coconut water

Combine all the ingredients in a blender and slowly bring the speed from low to high. Let the mixture blend for 30 seconds, until it is a beautiful shade of green with no hint of kale bits in it. Pour into a glass and garnish with a small piece of kale, if entertaining.

Recipe Notes:
*   **All these ingredients have amazing health benefits:**
*   **Kale contains antioxidants like vitamin C, beta-carotene, and manganese. Kale also provides us with at least forty-five different recently discovered flavonoids, including kaempferol and quercetin. Many of the flavonoids in kale are also now known to function not only as antioxidants but also as anti-inflammatory compounds.**
*   **Cucumber is full of B-complex vitamins, vitamin C, calcium, magnesium, and potassium, to name a few, and relieves stress by supporting your adrenal glands.**
*   **Mangoes contain over twenty vitamins and minerals, making them a superfood.**
*   **Coconut water is a good source of B-complex vitamins, such as folate, riboflavin, niacin, thiamin, and pyridoxine, which make it an excellent source of energy!**

x GF
x SF
x NF

MONKEY MILK
A QUICK, EASY
Smoothie Base

PREP + COOK TIME 2 MINUTES **MAKES** 1 (16-OUNCE) SERVING

1 cup frozen sliced organic
bananas

1 cup nondairy milk (sometimes
I freeze nondairy milk in
ice cube trays to make my
smoothie thicker)

In a blender, mix the bananas with the milk, starting on slow and gradually taking it to high. When the mixture is blended and uniform in color and texture, pour it into a glass and serve. Top with fresh bananas or a dash of cinnamon, if desired.

Recipe Notes:

If you enjoy a creamier smoothie, I recommend using a thicker milk, like coconut, hemp, or macadamia nut.

Also play around with the number of bananas to hit your taste buds. When freezing bananas, wait until they are very ripe to get as much taste and flavor as possible.

Bananas are powerhouses, containing the following nutrients:

- Potassium
- Vitamin B6
- Vitamin C
- Magnesium
- Copper
- Manganese
- Net carbohydrates
- Fiber
- Protein

X GF

X SF

X NF IF YOU USE HEMP,
COCONUT OR SEED MILK

Monkey Milk is nothing more than bananas and nondairy milk whipped up in a blender. Simple, yet so delish. The first time I had it was at a little raw café in California, and I was hooked. Being that I always have bananas in Hawaii, this smoothie has been a staple for my family at breakfast. It also serves as the base for endless smoothie possibilities. At different times, I've added kale, berries, other fruits, cocoa powder, protein powder, roots, spices, coffee, matcha, adaptogens, and even almond or peanut butter!

REJUVENATION WATERMELON
Fatigue Cure

The Fatigue Cure is watermelon and coconut water whipped up in a blender. Whether you are looking for a cure from a late night-out drinking, a stressful day, or a hard workout, this is the juice for you. This smoothie is filled with nutrients that will help your body heal.

PREP + COOK TIME 2 MINUTES **MAKES** 24 OUNCES 2-12 OUNCE

2 cups watermelon chunks

1 cup coconut water
(fresh is best)

In a blender, combine the watermelon and coconut water, starting on low and gradually taking it to high speed. Pour the mixture into a glass, drink, and see how much better you feel!

Recipe Note:
- **Pink watermelon is also a source of lycopene, a potent carotenoid antioxidant that helps neutralize free radicals in the body.**
- **Coconut water contains antioxidants that protect cells from damaging free radicals**

x GF
x SF
x NF

COLD BREW COFFEE

There are so many ways to make cold brew coffee. First, let me start with what it is and what its health benefits are. Cold brew coffee is just that—coffee brewed with cold water. It is almost raw . . . just the beans have been roasted. It can have as much as 70 percent less acidity than a regular brewed cup. It is thought that the reason people have problems digesting coffee is because of the high acidity. The benefits of cold brew coffee include no indigestion, heartburn, or acid reflux. I make my cold brew with high levels of caffeine (that is why we drink it, after all), and I feel better overall when I replace my hot cup with cold brew.

PREP + COOK TIME 8 TO 16 HOURS
MAKES 4 (16-OUNCE) OR 8 (8-OUNCE) SERVINGS

8 ounces ground coffee
64 ounces cold water

Combine the coffee and cold water in a ½-gallon Mason jar, and screw on the lid. Let it sit on the counter for 24 hours, shaking it when you pass by twice a day. Then, transfer the jar to the fridge and keep it there for 24 hours. Strain the coffee through a filter bag into a clean jar, and store it in the fridge for up to 3 weeks.

I enjoy my cold brew with coconut creamer and homemade simple syrup or maple syrup.

Recipe Note:
At home, I have a fancy machine, called a Yama, that does the work for me and makes a bunch at a time. I recommend it if you are a coffee connoisseur and looking for some eye candy for your counter. They are truly works of art! For the rest, this recipe will make amazing coffee every time.

X GF
X SF
X NF

WHERE DO YOU GET YOUR
Protein Shake?

I love protein shakes. They make it possible to get a filling fix on the go that is packed with vitamins and minerals. Normally, I have it once a day. When I am low on time or cleansing, I have two. I keep them simple, but you can add anything else, such as frozen fruits, nut butters, cacao nibs, nuts, or greens.

PREP + COOK TIME 2 MINUTES **MAKES** 1 (16-OUNCE) SERVING

2 cups nondairy milk
   (I use almond milk)
2 scoops vegan protein powder
   (I use chocolate)

Combine the milk and protein powder in a blender and blend for 20 to 30 seconds, until smooth. (If you do not have a blender or are short on time, you can shake it up in a Mason jar instead.)

Recipe Note:

I have my own shake powder called Hollan Hawaii Protein Powder, but you can use any brand you like! I recommend always looking at the label and making sure there aren't a lot of ingredients that you don't recognize. If you want to try mine, please order it online at hollanhawaii.com.

x **GF**
x **SF (if your protein powder is)**
x **NF (if you use hemp, coconut, or seed milk)**

CHEATER SODA: SPRITZ UP
Your life!

I was not raised with water as a norm in my house. I drank juice, soda, tea, and milk, but water was kind of foreign. It was not until I was in high school that water started becoming mainstream and bottled. As I started searching for health, I realized water was really missing from my life. So, I now tend to only drink water, but when I want something different and bubbly, I make this cheater soda.

PREP + COOK TIME 1 MINUTE **MAKES** 4 (8-OUNCE) SERVINGS

Ice
1 bottle (32 ounces)
 sparkling water
Liquid stevia
Lime and/or lemon wedges

Fill four tumblers almost to the top with ice. Pour in enough sparkling water to reach the top of each glass, add 4 drops of stevia to each glass, and squeeze in some lemon and/or lime juice. Garnish each glass with a lime or lemon wedge.

Recipe Note:
Play around with different variations:
- **Cream soda: take away the citrus and add ¼ teaspoon vanilla extract**
- **Root beer: add sarsaparilla and vanilla**
- **Grapefruit: replace the lemon/lime wedges with grapefruit**

X **GF**
X **SF**
X **NF**

FEEL THE BURN: GINGER SHOTS
for Immunity

I love ginger. It has so many health benefits, and I always feel instantly better when I eat it. At some point, I stopped taking alcoholic shots at the bar and replaced them with healthy shots. You can always dilute these if you prefer them lighter. I like to feel it burn and work its magic.

PREP + COOK TIME 5 MINUTES **MAKES** 2 (2-OUNCE) SHOTS

¼ **pound ginger, peeled if it looks rough and cut into chunks that will fit in your juicer**

Put the ginger pieces in your juicer and juice according to the manufacturer's directions. Take as a shot, 2 ounces at a time.

Recipe Notes
- A juicer works best for this recipe, but you can always use a blender, instead. Just put some water in your blender, add the ginger, blend on high speed, and strain.
- To make the shots less intense, dilute with water or lemon juice.
- Ginger is known to help with nausea, inflammation, and certain cancers. It is a powerhouse of antioxidants and is known to boost the immune system. I always say, a little ginger a day keeps the doctor away.

x GF
x SF
x NF

SUPERSTAR TURMERIC
Shots

Turmeric is amazing. It has anti-cancerous and anti-inflammatory properties and is good for your heart. That is a very short list of its magic. Turmeric grows abundantly in Hawaii, so I always have it at my fingertips. If you do not live in Hawaii, check for fresh turmeric at your local health foods market or specialty grocer.

PREP + COOK TIME 5 MINUTES **MAKES** 2 (2-OUNCE) SHOTS

¼ **pound fresh turmeric, peeled and cut into chunks that will fit in your juicer**

Put the turmeric pieces in your juicer and juice according to the manufacturer's directions. Take as a shot, 2 ounces at a time.

Recipe Notes:
- **A juicer is recommended for this recipe; however, if you have no juicer, you can always blend the turmeric with a little water and then strain it.**
- **To make the shots less intense, dilute with water or lemon juice.**
- **Research shows that black pepper helps your body better absorb the nutrients in turmeric, so maybe add a dash of freshly ground black pepper.**
- **Turmeric is the superstar of superfoods. It is a powerful weapon against inflammation that kicks free-radical butt. Turmeric helps boost your immune system, ease joint pain, protect your heart, treat and prevent cancer, heal your gut… the list of benefits goes on and on. Add this power shot to your daily routine, and watch your body transform.**

X **GF**
X **SF**
X **NF if you use hemp, coconut or seed milk**

I HEART BLUEBERRIES:
Banana-less Smoothie

I really do love blueberries. Whether enjoying them fresh or in this delightful smoothie, they are a norm in my life and self-care. They're full of antioxidants, and they always give me a burst of energy. I also drink a lot of smoothies, and I especially love the ones that are creamy without bananas. This has become my favorite creamy, banana-less smoothie. I make a smoothie bowl with the same base—see the note below!

PREP + COOK TIME 5 MINUTES **MAKES** 1 (16-OUNCE) SERVING

1 cup frozen blueberries

2 frozen coconut cubes (see note, below)

1 date (not frozen)

1 cup nondairy milk

In a blender, combine all the ingredients and blend for about 45 seconds, until smooth. Enjoy right away.

Recipe Notes:

- Coconut cubes are just frozen coconut milk. I use ice cube trays. They add a creamy, frozen touch to my smoothies.
- Blueberries have so many benefits. They are high in antioxidants, can help fight cancer, amp up weight loss, boost brain health, alleviate inflammation, support digestion, and promote heart health.
- To make a blueberry smoothie bowl, reduce the amount of milk to half, blend with the other ingredients, and top with fresh bananas and granola.

x GF

x SF

x NF (if you use hemp, coconut, or seed milk)

SPICE-ME-UP
Chai

Ohhhh, I love me some chai! Sweet, spicy, dreamy, and heartwarming. This drink is my go-to afternoon pick-me-up. The spices in chai tea have so many great benefits, like reducing blood sugar levels, aiding digestion, and possibly helping with weight loss too.

PREP + COOK TIME 5 MINUTES **MAKES** 1 (16-OUNCE) OR 2 (8-OUNCE) SERVINGS

2 whole cloves

2 cardamom pods, or ½ teaspoon cardamom powder

1 teaspoon powdered or grated fresh ginger

1 cinnamon stick, broken into pieces

⅛ teaspoon freshly ground black pepper

2 tablespoons organic sugar

2 tablespoons loose black tea

2 cups non dairy milk

With a mortar and pestle or in your blender or food processor, grind together the cloves, cardamom, and ginger. Transfer this and the rest of the ingredients to a medium saucepan over medium-low heat, and slowly bring the mixture to your preferred temperature. Use a whisk or fork to create froth on top. Strain the mixture through a tea strainer into mugs, and enjoy!

Recipe Notes:

- If you like it cold, follow the same recipe, but instead of milk add in ½ cup of water. Bring the mixture to a boil, then strain it into a pitcher or jar. Fill your mugs or glasses with ice, pour in the tea, and top with non dairy milk.

- You can always adjust the amounts of the spices if some are too strong or weak for your taste.

X GF

X SF (if the milk you use is soy free)

X NF (if you use hemp, coconut, or seed milk)

Matcha is truly amazing! It is green tea, but thicker, like coffee. The difference between green tea and matcha is that matcha is the entire leaf turned to powder form. It packs a punch of flavor that will remind you of green tea ice cream from your favorite Japanese restaurant.

Matcha tea originated as the ceremonial tea of temple high priests in Japan. The purpose of this tea was to enhance concentration before meditation. What I love about drinking matcha is that it has a slow release of caffeine, which does not cause you to crash in the middle of the day. It is full of antioxidants, and all studies point to a long list of benefits. In just one serving of matcha, there are substantial quantities of potassium, vitamins A and C, iron, protein, and calcium. I love when something that tastes so yummy supports your body and cells. When you mix it into a latte with hemp milk, you get a power punch of protein, too.

LOVE YOU MATCHA
latte!

PREP + COOK TIME 4 MINUTES **MAKES** 1 (16-OUNCE) SERVING

1-2 teaspoons matcha powder (depending on strength of matcha)

2 teaspoons organic sugar or pure maple syrup

¼ cup hot water

12 ounces hemp milk

If you have a matcha tea set, combine the matcha and sugar in the bowl, add the hot water, and whisk for 45 seconds, until smooth. If you do not have a matcha tea set, combine the matcha and sugar in a cereal bowl, add the hot water, and use a fork to whisk until smooth.

Heat the milk in a pan over medium heat and use the whisk (or a fork) to create a little foam. Heat until you the milk reaches your desired temperature. Pour the hot milk into a mug, stir in the matcha mixture, and enjoy.

Recipe Notes:
- **Matcha is a great replacement when you are trying to give up coffee. And, just like coffee, there are so many varieties of matcha that you need to try different brands until you find the one that suits your taste buds. I recommend leaning toward ceremonial grade matcha that has a vibrant green color, rather than a yellow/brownish color. Also, find one that originates in Japan and ranges around the packaging size of 30 grams.**
- **As you see in the picture, we use a ceremonial matcha tea set, which contains a bamboo whisk, bamboo scooper, and a small ceramic bowl. Making your matcha latte this way brings a traditional ritual to your morning.**
- **Adjust the sugar amount to your liking.**
- **During warm months, do not heat the milk. Fill your mug with ice, pour in the milk, and then add the matcha.**

x GF

x SF (if you don't use soy milk)

x NF (if you use hemp, coconut, or seed milk)

I AM BORED WITH WATER

Mint Tea

Sometimes I get bored with water, but I still need to stay hydrated. So, I liven myself up with something that quenches my thirst. Enter, mint tea—refreshing, delicious, and super supportive of your digestion. Not to mention, it contains zero sugar and little to no calories.

PREP + COOK TIME 10-15 MINUTES **MAKES** 1 QUART

**3 organic mint tea bags,
   or ½ cup fresh mint leaves**
2 cups boiling water
2 cups cold water

Place the tea bags or mint leaves in a tea pot or saucepan, and pour in the boiling water. Cover and let steep for 30 to 45 minutes. Remove the tea bags or strain the tea into a pitcher. Add the cold water. Serve over ice or store the tea in the fridge for up to a week. Drink throughout your day.

Recipe Note:

Mint also promotes digestion and soothes the stomach in case of indigestion or inflammation. When your stomach feels sick, drinking a cup of mint tea can give you relief.

X GF
X SF
X N

SQUEEZE ME, PLEASE
Hawaiian Lemonade

Trust me—this will be a big hit at any summer beach party. Friends and family of all ages will be refreshed and impressed. It is tart, sweet, and creamy. (Yes, creamy!) Close your eyes, and it will take you away to the cool trade winds of Hawaii.

PREP + COOK TIME 5 MINUTES **MAKES** 6 CUPS

2 cups hot water

1½ cups sugar

**2 cups freshly squeezed
lemon juice**

**¼ cup canned
coconut milk**

2 cups cold water

Mix together the hot water and sugar in a pitcher, stirring until the sugar dissolves. Add the lemon juice and coconut milk, and then pour in enough cold water to reach the top of the pitcher. Cover and refrigerate for up to a week. Stir well (the coconut milk will settle at the top), and serve over ice, garnished with lemon slices.

Recipe Note:

You're in luck when life gives you lemons, because these fruits have such great nutritional benefits. Lemons are alkalizing for your body, rich in vitamin C, amazing for your liver, and full of other vitamins, minerals, phytonutrients, and antioxidants.

x **GF**

x **SF**

x **NF**

BREKKY
ITEMS

Rethink Breakfast

SACRED

Scones

PREP + COOK TIME 30 MINUTES **MAKES** 10 SCONES

1¾ cups gluten-free flour

⅔ cup gluten-free rolled oats

⅓ cup sugar

¼ teaspoon salt

2 teaspoons baking powder

½ teaspoon baking soda

½ cup cold vegan butter

⅔ cup nondairy milk
(I prefer almond milk)

⅔ cup chopped fruit (fresh,
frozen, or dried), in small
bite-size pieces

Preheat the oven to 400°F. Line a baking sheet
with parchment.

Whisk together the flour, oats, sugar, salt, baking powder,
and baking soda in a large bowl. Cut the butter into
small pieces with a fork and add it to the flour mixture,
along with the milk. Stir slowly until the butter and milk
are incorporated. The batter should be crumbly, not a
uniform-looking paste. Add the fruit and fold until just
incorporated. If it seems too wet, add in a little more
flour; if it seems too dry, add a little more milk. It should
resemble bread dough. If you have a mixer, let it do all the
hard work for you.

Transfer the dough to a lightly floured counter. Form it
into a round loaf, then use a sharp knife to cut it into 8 pie
slices. Gently transfer the wedges to the prepared baking
sheet, and bake for 15 to 20 minutes, until golden brown.
Let the scones cool slightly, and enjoy them warm with
vegan butter or vegan whipped cream.

x **GF**

x **SF (if using soy free butter)**

x **NF (if you use hemp, coconut, or seed milk)**

There is something special about the mixture of flour, sugar, and butter. To me, it's pure joy. This is my spin on the famous English pastry. I make my scones gluten-free with very little sugar so that they are also guilt-free. Have fun—add vegan chocolate chips if you are feeling chocolatey, ginger if you are feeling spicy, or anything that will bring you bliss.

HOMEY
Roasted Potatoes

I pray that potatoes are a good carb, so I always tell my body they are nourishing. I do not want to live a life where potatoes are not involved. These are good for breakfast, in place of fries, on top of any salad, for dinner, or just as a snack. In my house, there is always ketchup involved and a lot of happy faces, because everyone in my family enjoys them. I always have them on the side with my tofu scramble and toast. I also use this recipe for my Killer Quesadilla (page 88). I can't explain how versatile this recipe is, and how many different meals you can use this as a base for.

PREP + COOK TIME 30 MINUTES **SERVES** 4

2 pounds red skinned potatoes, cut into ½-inch dice

2 tablespoons olive oil

1 tablespoon salt

Freshly ground black pepper (optional)

Preheat the oven to 450°F. Line a rimmed baking sheet with parchment.

In a large bowl, combine the potatoes, olive oil, and salt, and stir until the potatoes are evenly coated. I do not use black pepper here, but if you love it, add some in. Spread the potatoes on the prepared baking sheet, and bake for 30 minutes, flipping them halfway through, until they are golden brown and tender in the middle.

Recipe Notes:
Red potatoes are particularly healthy because of the nutritious skin. The skin alone contains fiber, B vitamins, iron, and potassium.

x GF

x SF

x NF

I CAN'T BELIEVE
IT'S NOT EGGS

Tofu Scramble

PREP + COOK TIME 30 MINUTES **SERVES** 4

1 tablespoon olive oil

¼ onion, diced

½ red or orange bell pepper, diced

½ cup diced zucchini

½ bunch kale, stemmed and chopped

24 ounces firm to extra-firm tofu

½ to 1 teaspoon curry and/or turmeric powder

2 tablespoons tamari

Salt and freshly ground black pepper

Heat the olive oil in a skillet over medium heat, and add the onion, bell pepper, and zucchini. Stir every minute so the vegetables do not stick to the pan. While they cook, crumble the tofu with your hands into a bowl; it should look like scrambled eggs.

Once your veggies are sautéed golden, add kale here with the tofu crumbles and then turn the heat to medium low. Once all the water evaporates, add in curry the and tamari, and stir until the mixture looks like an egg scramble. Season with salt and pepper, and serve.

Recipe Notes:

Although it has curry in it, this dish does not have a curry taste. The spice is used mainly for color. You can always adjust or omit the curry powder, or use turmeric instead.

x **GF (if you use gluten-free toast)**

x **SF (if you use cauliflower**

instead of tofu and sub salt for tamari)

x **NF**

I love weekends, because they are prime time for breakfasts and brunches. That's when family gathers around the table to have a meal together, relax, and catch up. Growing up, I loved scrambled eggs with cheese and house potatoes with buttered toast. When I first went vegan, I had a hard time finding meals to replace the original, and then I started experimenting with tofu. It is my go-to big breakfast, and one that will even leave non-vegan guests happy. I serve it with Homey Roasted Potatoes (page 67) and toast slathered in vegan butter.

My kids do not all like oatmeal, but they all LOVE oatmeal pancakes. This is a great way to get a wholesome grain in the morning, but still feel like you just ate something naughty. I always serve them with vegan butter and maple syrup. For fun, add chocolate chips, goji berries, or bananas—GO WILD!

YOU WILL FALL FOR THESE
Pumpkin Oat Pancakes

PREP + COOK TIME 20 MINUTES **SERVES** 4

3 cups gluten-free oat flour
(I make my own by throwing
4 cups rolled oats in the
blender.)

1 tablespoon baking powder

1 teaspoon salt

1 cup pumpkin purée
(You can roast your own and
purée it, or use canned.)

2 cups water, plus more as
needed

1 cup nondairy milk

Olive oil or vegan butter,
for greasing the skillet

Vegan butter and pure
maple syrup, for topping

x GF
x SF (if you use soy
free butter)
x NF (if you use
hemp, coconut, or
seed milk)

Combine the flour, baking powder, salt, pumpkin purée, water, and milk in a large bowl or the bowl of an electric mixer; mix with a wooden spoon or the paddle attachment until a smooth batter forms. Let it sit for a few minutes. If the batter seems too stiff, add more water until it is pourable.

Place a large skillet over medium-low heat and add a little oil or butter. When the oil is hot or the butter has melted, spoon batter into the skillet to make pancakes of your desired size. When the batter starts to bubble all over, flip the pancakes and cook on the other side for 3-4 minutes or until lightly brown. Voila! Healthy pancakes.

Serve hot, topped with vegan butter and maple syrup.

Recipe Notes:
- This recipe is so yummy, but I want you to play around. Use different gluten-free flours instead of oat flour, or, if you are not gluten-free, use all-purpose flour. Substitute more milk for the pumpkin if you want regular pancakes, or mash a cup of banana and use it instead of pumpkin for banana pancakes.
- Oats are high in the soluble fiber beta-glucan, which has numerous benefits. It helps reduce cholesterol and blood sugar levels, promotes healthy gut bacteria, and increases feelings of fullness.

WORLD'S BEST BANANA Bread

I honestly believe this banana bread recipe could win awards. Customers always praised it. I came up with the recipe years ago, and I still am not bored of eating it. It wows me every time.

PREP + COOK TIME 1 HOUR **SERVES** 1
MAKES (8.5" X 4.5" X 2.75" INCH) LOAF OR 4 MINI LOAVES

½ cup olive oil, plus more for
    greasing the pan(s)
3 cups brown rice flour, plus
    more for coating the pan(s)
4½ pounds whole bananas,
    roughly 3 pounds peeled and
    mashed
1 cup water
1 cup organic sugar
3 teaspoons baking soda
1 teaspoon xanthan gum
½ teaspoon salt

Preheat the oven to 375°F. Grease the loaf pan(s) with oil and either line with parchment or dust with rice flour.

Place the mashed bananas in the bowl of an electric mixer, and add the water and oil. Slowly mix in the flour, sugar, baking soda, xanthan gum, and salt. Pour the batter into the prepared loaf pan(s).

Bake for 45 minutes (less if mini-pans) or until a toothpick inserted in the center comes out clean. (I tend to let it go longer than I think, as I like it better darker and more bread-like. As my teacher in pastry school said, "It should look like it spent too much time in the sun.")

Recipe Notes:
* **This dough also makes the most splendid pancakes. Just add one more cup of water and cook in a skillet over medium heat. Serve with vegan butter and maple syrup.**
* **Bananas have a high fiber content. They are loaded with both soluble and insoluble fiber.**

x GF
x SF (if using soy-free
butter)
x NF

HERBY AVOCADO *Toast*

It seems like everyone is obsessed with avocado toast these days. You can have it anywhere, from Hawaii to New York, and it is not just on vegan menus. Oh, and can we talk health benefits? Avocados are a naturally nutrient-rich food and contain nearly twenty vitamins and minerals. They are also packed with monounsaturated fatty acids. Yay!

PREP + COOK TIME 10 MINUTES **SERVES** 2

4 slices of your favorite bread (gluten-free or not)

2 tablespoons Herb Oil (see page 188) or vegan butter

1 large or 2 small ripe avocados, sliced

Salt and freshly ground black pepper

½ cup clover sprouts

8 cherry tomatoes, halved

Toast the bread and drizzle each slice with some of the herb oil (save some for drizzling over top). Or butter (see side note). Next, on each slice of toast, arrange one-fourth of the avocado, and smoosh the avocado with a fork until it looks mashed. Cut each toast in half on a diagonal, and sprinkle with salt and pepper. Top with clover sprouts and cherry tomatoes. Serve or drizzle with herb oil.

Recipe Notes:

- **This recipe is so versatile. Try swapping out the herb oil for vegan butter. Love pickled foods? Top it with pickled radishes and microgreens. Do something crazy.**
- **Avocados are packed with vitamin K, folate, vitamin c, potassium, vitamins B5 and B6, and vitamin E. They contain small amounts of magnesium, manganese, copper, iron, zinc, phosphorous, and vitamins A, B1 (thiamine), B2 (riboflavin), and B3 (niacin). They are like a multivitamin from nature.**

x GF (if you use gluten-free bread)

x SF

x NF

OUI OUI
FRENCH
Toast

PREP + COOK TIME 20 MINUTES **SERVES** 4

8 slices of bread (sourdough,
    baguette, whole wheat, or
    whatever else you like)
½ cup all-purpose flour
1 cup almond milk, or any
    nondairy milk
1 teaspoon ground cinnamon,
    plus more for dusting
2 tablespoons pure maple
    syrup, plus more for serving
1 teaspoon vegan butter, plus
    more for serving
Berries, for serving

Slice the bread as desired. In a pie dish, whisk together the flour, milk, cinnamon, and maple syrup.

Melt the butter in a large skillet over medium-low heat. Dip the bread slices into the batter and cook them, a few at a time, for about 3 minutes per side or until they are golden brown. (If you love cinnamon, like me, sprinkle a little bit on the bread before you flip it.) Repeat with the rest of the bread and batter.

Serve the French toast topped with vegan butter, maple syrup, and fresh berries.

Recipe Notes:

Pure maple syrup contains numerous antioxidants, gets a lower score on the glycemic index, fights inflammatory diseases, may help protect against cancer, helps protect skin, is a healthy alternative to sugar for improved digestion, and supplies the body with important vitamins and minerals.

x **GF (if you use gluten-free bread and gluten-free flour)**
x **SF (if you use soy-free butter)**
x **NF (if you use hemp, coconut, or seed milk)**

Say oui to French toast, and no to eggs and cream. I read somewhere once that French toast was originally vegan, because we did not always have an abundance of eggs and cow's milk. This recipe never feels like something is missing. The best part of all: you probably have all the ingredients in your pantry.

LEGGO YOUR GUILT
Waffles

PREP + COOK TIME 30 MINUTES **SERVES** 6 WAFFLES

2 cups brown rice flour
¼ cup sugar
1 teaspoon baking powder
1 teaspoon xanthan gum
½ teaspoon salt
2 cups almond milk
Cooking spray or
  cooking oil

Preheat your waffle iron.

In a medium bowl, mix together the flour, sugar, baking powder, xanthan gum, and salt. Pour in the milk and stir until smooth.

Spray the preheated waffle iron with nonstick cooking spray and sprinkle with a little rice flour. Pour some of the batter into the waffle iron, seal it, and cook until golden brown. Remember to grease the iron with cooking spray between batches. If your waffles keep getting stuck, try using a chopstick in the corners to pop them out.

Serve the waffles with vegan butter and maple syrup. If you have any berries, throw them on top, too.

Recipe Notes:

Sometimes I make churro waffles by dipping them in melted vegan butter and then coating them with cinnamon sugar.

x **GF**
x **SF**
x **NF (if you use hemp, coconut, or seed milk)**

I want my kids' diet to seem normal, even though we eat vegan, so I try to make traditional foods as healthy as they can be. I love these waffles with fresh slices of banana and a drizzle of maple syrup. They're crisp on the outside and fluffy on the inside. With this easy, healthy recipe, you can toss the boxed stuff and make your waffles from scratch. You can also freeze the finished waffles, then pop them in the toaster oven whenever you need a quick breakfast or snack.

DIY GLUTEN-FREE

Granola

Eat it as a snack, on açai bowls, or in place of cereal with almond milk and sliced banana. Granola is often pricey at the market, but it is very easy to make, so there's no reason not to keep it stocked at home.

PREP + COOK TIME 30 MINUTES **MAKES** 2½ POUNDS

1 (2-pound) bag organic gluten-free rolled oats (not instant oatmeal)

1 cup brown rice flour

¾ teaspoon salt

¾ cup pure maple syrup

⅔ cup olive oil

½ cup brown rice syrup

1 cup dried fruit, nuts, and/or chocolate chips (optional)

Preheat the oven to 325°F.

Mix all the ingredients together in a bowl, and spread the mixture evenly on two parchment-lined baking sheets.

Bake for 15 minutes, mix it around, and increase the oven temperature to 350°F. Bake until golden, about 10 to 15 minutes. Depending on how you like your granola (crunchy or softer), play around with cooking time. Let it cool before transferring it to an airtight container.

Recipe Notes:
Remember oats can lower cholesterol levels and protect LDL cholesterol from damage.

x **GF**
x **SF**
x **NF**

KEEP IT LIGHT TO KEEP IT TIGHT

Fruit Salad

It is so warm most of the time in Hawaii. We have such an amazing tropical fruit season that it is hard to not fall in love with eating fruit. Fruit salad is good for breakfast, lunch, a snack, dinner, and dessert. This local mix is our favorite fruit salad combo, and it gets yummier the longer it stays in the fridge (it keeps for up to 3 days). Of course, play around with what you like and what is in season.

PREP + COOK TIME 15 MINUTES **SERVES** 6

1 mango, diced

1 papaya, diced

½ Thai watermelon, cut into large dice

1 apple, chopped

2 bananas, sliced

2 oranges, roughly chopped

Squeeze of fresh lime juice

Finely sliced fresh mint

Coconut whipped cream, for topping (optional)

Mix the fruit in a large bowl and add the lime juice and mint. Serve in bowls. If you are serving it for dessert, top with dollops of coconut whipped cream.

Recipe Notes:

Fruits are particularly high in many vitamins and minerals and are also full of water; so, they are naturally hydrating.

x **GF**

x **SF**

x **NF**

AÇAI SUPER
Bowl

Açai berries are one of the top superfoods, as they have amazing health benefits. Açai decays very quickly once it is picked from its palm tree, so you normally find it in frozen purée packets or dried. I use the packets. I am lucky to have a company here in Kauai, Tambor Açai, that imports the berries from Brazil. Tambor Açai is pure acai without additives and sugar, and they deliver straight to your door. This is my family's favorite.

PREP + COOK TIME 6 MINUTES **SERVES** 1

1½ **frozen acai packets,
     cut in half**
1 cup **frozen sliced bananas**
½ cup **nondairy milk
     (I use homemade
     macadamia nut milk)**

Place all the ingredients in a high-speed blender, and secure the lid and tamper attachment (stick).

Slowly start to blend on low and gradually bring it up to high. Using the stick, move the ingredients around until it resembles sorbet consistency. Then, use a silicone spatula to transfer it to a bowl. Top with sliced fresh banana and ¼ cup homemade granola (see page 81), and enjoy.

Recipe Notes:

- **You can make so many variations by bringing in toppings or adding to your base, such as: goji berries, hemp seeds, chia seeds, macadamia nuts, almonds, fresh fruit, chocolate chips, cacao nibs, peanut butter, almond butter, and more as toppings. Blend-ins include chlorella, spirulina, kale, greens, maca root, peanut butter, and almond butter.**
- **Açai berries are beneficial for the heart, skin, and digestion. They are good for weight loss and cellular metabolism. The antioxidants in açai berries are intense and effective in slowing the aging process, as well as fighting cancer. They can increase blood flow and are even said to be a natural aphrodisiac.**

x **GF**

x **SF**

x **NF (if you use hemp, coconut, or seed milk)**

LUNCH
BRUNCH
My favorite meal

KILLER
Quesadilla

Whenever I have leftover Homey Roasted Potatoes (page 67) hanging around in the fridge, I love whipping up a batch of these quesadillas. You can enjoy them with salsa or vegan sour cream, but they are also tasty as is.

PREP + COOK TIME 15 MINUTES **SERVES** 4

1 tablespoon olive oil, for the pan

¼ cup diced red bell pepper

¼ cup diced onion

2 cups leftover Homey Roasted Potatoes (see page 67)

Salt and freshly ground black pepper

6 flour or corn tortillas

Heat olive oil in a skillet over medium heat, add the pepper and onion, and cook for 2 minutes, until golden. Add the homey potatoes and mash them lightly with a fork into the onion and pepper mix. Cook for about 4 minutes, until warmed through. Transfer to a bowl and set aside.

Scoop ½ cup of the potato mixture onto one side of each tortilla, and fold the tortilla over the filling to seal. Lower the heat to medium low and add the remaining tablespoon olive oil to the skillet. Cook the quesadillas one at a time, until they are golden brown on both sides. Transfer to a plate and keep warm.

Cut each quesadilla into four pieces, and serve warm. I top mine with vegan sour cream and clover sprouts and serve with refried beans on the side.

x **GF (if you use corn tortillas)**

x **SF**

x **NF**

HOW TO FALL IN LOVE WITH
Kale Salad

This is so tasty. You won't believe that it is as simple as it is. For this recipe, I top the kale with papayas and crushed macadamia nuts. You can give this a try or add other fruits, veggies, nuts, and seeds to top it! I suggest using whatever is local to you, to ensure quality of taste. Besides, buying locally is more sustainable.

PREP + COOK TIME 10 MINUTES WITH DRESSING,
5 MINUTES WITHOUT **SERVES** 4

1 bunch kale, stemmed and
   chopped (for softer texture,
   massage the leaves until they
   soften)
¼ cup Mac Nut Vinaigarette
   (see page 190)
1 papaya, peeled and cubed
   (about 1 cup)
¼ cup chopped macadamia
   nuts

In a bowl, toss the kale with the dressing, then transfer it to a platter and top with the papaya and macadamia nuts.

Recipe Notes:

At just 33 calories, one cup of raw kale has nearly 3 grams of protein; 2.5 grams of fiber (which helps manage blood sugar and makes you feel full); vitamins A, C, and K; Folate (a B vitamin that's key for brain development); and alpha-linolenic acid (an omega-3 fatty acid).

X GF
X SF Make a soy free version
   of dressing
X NF

THERE'S NO FAKIN' ... IT'S YUMMIER THAN *Bacon BLT*

This is a play on the classic BLT, but with a few substitutes . . . guess which! Make it with your favorite bread, and this is a home run. I eat it a lot more than I ever did the original sandwich, and it was also a very popular item on the menu at the café.

PREP + COOK TIME 20 MINUTES **SERVES** 4

8 bread slices, toasted

Vegan mayo

1 or 2 tomatoes (depending on size), cut into 8 slices

8 leafs of red leaf lettuce

Clover sprouts

12 slices Oink-less Bacon (recipe follows)

Lay the bread slices on a cutting board. For each sandwich, spread both bread slices with mayo, then layer with tomato, lettuce, sprouts, and bacon. Slice on the diagonal, and enjoy!

x GF (if you use gluten-free bread)

x NF

x SF (if you use soy-free bacon)

OINK-LESS
Bacon

I don't remember exactly what bacon tastes like. I do know, however, that this version replaces bacon in any recipe bacon is called for. It is smoky and savory, and it adds so much flavor to BLTs and other recipes. I use it to top soups and salads, add it to baked beans, and love snacking on it straight from the pan. I give you the option of using tempeh, eggplant, or coconut meat. Try them all and see which one you like best.

SERVES 4 (MAKES 12 SLICES) **TOTAL PREP TIME** 20 MINUTES

For the marinade:
2 tablespoons olive oil
2 tablespoons tamari
1 tablespoon vegan Worcestershire sauce
1 tablespoon pure maple syrup or brown sugar
2 teaspoons liquid smoke
½ teaspoon smoked paprika
Red pepper flakes (optional)
½ pound of tempeh, eggplant, or fresh coconut meat

Preheat the oven to 325°F.
Mix all the marinade ingredients together with a spoon in a small bowl. Set aside.

To make the "bacon," slice the tempeh, eggplant, or coconut lengthwise so it resembles bacon strips. Place the strips in a baking dish, and pour the marinade over the top. Cover and let the "bacon" marinate in the refrigerator for 2 hours. (If you're in a hurry, you can always just brush on the marinade and bake the "bacon" right away, but if you have the time, marinating makes a big flavor difference.)

Bake the "bacon" for 20 minutes, until the marinade is all soaked up. (Like it crispier? Bake it longer.)

CURRY NO-CHICKEN
Salad

There are certain things I thought I had given up when I went vegan, and curry chicken salad was one of them. That is, until Beyond Meat came out with super tasty vegan chicken strips. I first had this recipe at Whole Foods in Los Angeles, and right away I knew I needed to recreate it to share with my friends and family back home.

PREP + COOK TIME 10 MINUTES **SERVES** 4

½ **cup raisins**

⅓ **cup vegan mayo**

3 **green onions, chopped**

1½ **teaspoons curry powder**

½ **teaspoon salt**

2 **tablespoons pure
   maple syrup**

1 **(9-ounce) package
   Beyond Meat chicken strips**

Combine everything except the chicken strips in a large bowl. Mix well with a whisk. Once everything is combined, add the chicken strips and fold them in with a rubber spatula. Serve the salad on a bed of mixed greens or kale, in a sandwich, or straight from the bowl.

Recipe Notes:

Beyond Meat is precooked, so no need to heat it first! You can buy it at Whole Foods, Sprouts, and local health food stores.

x **GF**

x **SF with soy free vegan mayo
and soy free chicken strips**

x **NF**

SAN FRAN AVO

Sub Sandy

Growing up in San Francisco, deli sandwiches were my absolute favorite. Not only were there sandwich shops sprinkled everywhere, but the bread in SF is to die for. My personal favorite is a sourdough roll, but you can pick your favorite roll or slices and make this sandwich your own. Add what you like and omit what you do not.

PREP + COOK TIME 10 MINUTES **SERVES** 2

4 slices of bread or 2 deli rolls, split
2 tablespoons vegan mayo
1 tablespoon yellow or Dijon mustard
1 large or 2 small avocados, sliced
1 tomato, sliced
8 leaves romaine lettuce
¼ small red onion sliced
8 pickle slices
Salt and freshly ground black pepper

Place the bread on a cutting board, and spread 1 tablespoon mayo and ½ tablespoon mustard on each roll or each of 2 slices of bread. Start stacking each sandwich with avocado, tomato, lettuce, onion, and pickles. Season with salt and pepper. Cut in half and enjoy with chips and a salad.

X **GF (if you use gluten-free bread)**
X **SF (if you use soy-free vegan mayo)**
X **NF**

TAKE ME BACK

Comfort Bowl

This takes me to a place of total comfort. It is hearty and warm. It is salty and sweet. It reminds me of Thanksgiving, but with BBQ sauce instead of cranberries. You can always add or take away any of the toppings you do not love. Do yourself a favor, and make it on a rainy day.

PREP + COOK TIME 20 MINUTES **SERVES** 4

1 tablespoon extra-virgin olive oil

½ onion, sliced

½ cup mushrooms, sliced

1 small bag frozen corn, thawed

1 bunch kale, stemmed and chopped

1 teaspoon salt

½ teaspoon freshly ground black pepper

3 cups leftover mashed potatoes warmed

1 cup BBQ sauce, homemade (page200) or your favorite jar

Place a skillet over medium heat, and add the olive oil. When the oil is hot, add the onion and cook for 1 minute. Add the mushrooms and sauté for 1 minute, add the corn and cook it for 2 minutes, and then add the kale. Season with the salt and pepper. Cook for 2 more minutes, then take the skillet off the heat.

When you're ready to eat, divide the mashed potatoes among 4 bowls and top each serving with some sautéed veggies and a drizzle of BBQ sauce.

X GF

X SF

X NF

SUMMER SALADS

It's always summer in Hawaii

HAWAIIAN
Mac Daddy Salad

Hawaii really does love macaroni salad. It is the Mac Daddy of sides on most plate lunches. However, since the traditional version is rather unhealthy, I reworked the recipe, made it gluten-free and vegan, added a little more carrots and celery, and presto! A healthier macaroni salad for your bod.

PREP + COOK TIME 30 MINUTES **SERVES** 4

8 ounces brown rice elbow macaroni

¾ cup vegan mayo

1 tablespoon freshly squeezed lemon juice

1 teaspoon dried dill

½ teaspoon salt

¼ teaspoon freshly ground black pepper

½ cup minced carrots

½ cup minced celery

¼ cup minced onion

Cook the pasta according to the package directions. Drain, let it cool, and chill it in the fridge.

In a large bowl, mix together the vegan mayo, lemon juice, dill, salt, and pepper. Next, add the carrots, celery, onions, and then the pasta. Fold all ingredients together. Add more vegan mayo if you like it creamier. Taste and add more salt and pepper to your liking.

Recipe Notes:

- I serve this as a side at lunch or dinner and sometimes on top of greens as a meal of its own.
- To make it easier, you can mince the carrot, celery, and onion in your food processor.

x GF

x SF (if you use soy-free vegan mayo)

x NF

DA BEST
Potato Salad

I am a potato salad kind of girl. It is literally one of my favorite things. I love it as a side, on bread, on a cracker, for any meal . . . and I love all types. I adapted this one from a recipe from my BFF's mom, who was not vegan. Now, I enjoy it without the guilt, and it is a healthy pleasure. Eat it in a bowl on its own or as a side; it also makes great picnic food!

PREP + COOK TIME 30 MINUTES **SERVES** 4

1½ **pounds red-skinned potatoes**
¾ **cup vegan mayo**
2 **tablespoons pickle juice**
2 **tablespoons chopped fresh dill**
1 **teaspoon salt**
½ **teaspoon freshly ground black pepper**
1 **celery rib, diced**
2 **tablespoons minced red onion**
¼ **cup black olives sliced**
¼ **cup diced dill pickles (sweet or dill, your choice)**

Bring a large pot of water to a boil. Cut the potatoes into 1-inch cubes, keeping the skin on. Add them to the boiling water and boil for about 15 minutes, until they are tender (check with a knife). Drain well and rinse under cold water to stop the cooking. Chill potatoes in fridge.

Mix the vegan mayo, pickle juice, dill, salt, and pepper in a large bowl with a whisk. Add the celery, onion, olives, and pickles; toss well. Add the chilled potatoes, and stir again. If you want it creamier, add more vegan mayo.

X **GF**
X **SF (if you use soy-free vegan mayo)**
X **NF**

ALL CHOPPED UP
Yummy Salad

I am always eating salad. It is one of my go to foods because it's healthy, yummy, and there are so many variations you can make. But this recipe is one of my all time favorites because by chopping everything small you get bites of most of the ingredients in every bite. I serve it with my Homemade Ranch Dressing. This salad is yummy, dreamy, and creamy. You can change it up to include your favorite salad toppings, I stick with the basics.

PREP + COOK TIME 30 MINUTES **SERVES** 4

8 oz of your favorite lettuce. I use local organic mixed greens and tear the lettuce to bite sized pieces

1 carrot peeled and chopped finely

½ cucumber chopped finely

½ avocado chopped

¼ cup cherry tomatoes chopped

½ oz clover sprouts

Ranch Dressing (see page 191)

Put greens in a bowl or on a platter, top with the rest of the ingredients and serve with Ranch Dressing.

X **GF**

X **SF (if you use soy-free vegan mayo)**

X **NF**

ALL HAIL THIS
Vegan Caesar

I do not know if I ever had a Caesar salad before I was vegan. My friends all love it, but I was freaked out by anchovies. I do, however, remember my first vegan Caesar salad at Café Gratitude. It was life-changing. Light but filling, crunchy and bready, with a creamy dressing and a hint of lemon. This is my take on a classic Caesar.

PREP + COOK TIME TOTAL PREP TIME: 15 MINUTES WITH DRESSING, 10 MINUTES WITHOUT **SERVES** 4

For the croutons:

4 slices of your favorite bread, cut into ½ inch pieces

1 tablespoon olive oil

½ teaspoon salt

¼ teaspoon freshly ground black pepper

For the salad:

2 heads romaine or 10 heads baby romaine

1 lemon, cut into quarters

Sprinkle of nutritional yeast

Freshly ground black pepper

1 cup Cashew Caesar Dressing, see page 192

x **GF (if you make croutons from gluten-free bread)**

x **SF**

Preheat the oven to 400°F, and line a baking sheet with parchment.

In a large bowl, toss the bread pieces with the olive oil, salt, and pepper. Transfer the coated bread to the prepared baking sheet and bake for 10 to 15 minutes, until the croutons are golden and crunchy. Set aside to cool.

Cut the romaine either into quarters (wedges) or bite-sized pieces. (I like both ways; you cannot go wrong.) Put the lettuce in a salad bowl or on a plate.

Just before serving, drizzle the lettuce with the dressing. Place lemons on the plate or in the bowl for extra flavor. Sprinkle with nutritional yeast, and top with the croutons.

Recipe Notes:

A dieter's dream, romaine lettuce has about 8 calories and 1 to 2 grams of carbohydrates per cup. Although it's low in fiber, it is high in minerals, such as calcium, phosphorous, magnesium, and potassium.

WE GOT THE
Beet Salad

This is a raw, delish, nutrient-packed salad that would have made Popeye stronger than ever. The flavors have a power punch that's surprisingly strong for how simple it is.

PREP + COOK TIME TOTAL PREP TIME: 15 MINUTES WITH DRESSING, 5 MINUTES WITHOUT **SERVES** 2

6 ounces microgreens

1 large raw beet, peeled and thinly sliced

1 avocado, sliced

¼ cup Simple Dressing (see page 197)

Arrange the greens, beet slices, and avocado on a plate or bowl, and drizzle the dressing over the top.

Recipe Notes:

Beets are high in immune-boosting vitamin C, fiber, and essential minerals like potassium (essential for healthy nerve and muscle function) and manganese (good for your bones, liver, kidneys, and pancreas).

X GF
X SF
X NF

ENDLESS
Summer Rolls

There's always summer weather in Hawaii, so we serve summer rolls all year long. I love that summer rolls are just salad that's made more substantial by being wrapped up in rice paper. These were a huge seller at the café, and people rave about how fresh they are and how much they love the peanut sauce with them. They are commonly eaten for lunch, but I enjoy them as breakfast, too.

PREP + COOK TIME 15 MINUTES WITH DRESSING,
5 MINUTES WITHOUT **MAKES** 6 ROLLS

6 spring roll wrappers
½ cup shredded carrots
12 ounces mixed salad greens
2 cups shredded Napa cabbage
¼ cup finely shredded red cabbage
2 tablespoons chopped fresh mint
Peanut Sauce (see page 114), for dipping

Fill a wide, shallow bowl with cool water. One at a time, dip the wrappers in the water for a few seconds, shake off the excess water, and lay the wrappers on a clean surface.

In the middle of each wrap, make a line of 2 teaspoons carrot, a small handful of greens, 1/3 cup Napa cabbage, a little red cabbage, and a sprinkling of mint. To roll, fold one side over the pile of greens, tuck it under, and then roll it up tightly. Let the rolls sit for 1 minute before serving. Serve whole or cut in half with peanut sauce on the side.

Recipe Notes:
There are so many ways to enjoy spring roll wraps, so feel free to replace any ingredients with anything that strikes you as delicious.

x **GF**
x **SF**
x **NF (if you omit the peanut sauce)**

TAKE ME TO
Mexico Taco Salad

My take on taco salad is not that Mexican, it is just my rendition of different things from Mexican cuisine I enjoy over a salad. This is super delicious and filling. You can make it simply as a meal or turn it into a buffet dinner party. All ingredients are interchangeable with what you have or don't have. I serve it with either Hawaiian Island Dressing (page 196) or Chipotle Cream (page 201). De nada!

PREP + COOK TIME TOTAL PREP TIME: 15 MINUTES WITH DRESSING, 5 MINUTES WITHOUT **SERVES** 4

1 head green lettuce, shredded

1 carrot, peeled and chopped

1 cucumber, chopped

1 celery rib, diced

1 tomato, diced

1 green onion, diced

1 papaya, cut into half-inch pieces

1 (15-ounce) can black beans, drained, rinsed and then warmed

16 ounces tortilla chips, crushed

1 cup Hawaiian Island Dressing (see page 196) or Chipotle Cream (see page 201)

Put the greens in a large salad bowl and top with the carrot, cucumber, celery, tomato, green onion, papaya, and beans. Top with the chips, and serve either dressing on the side.

X GF

X SF with soy-free vegan mayo

X NF

IT'S ALWAYS
Summer Coleslaw

Sweet, creamy, and tangy—this is like sunshine! Serve it all by itself, as a side, on a sandwich, or on a burger. The crunch it will add to your soft sandwich is a perfect contrast of taste and texture. Bring this easy, breezy dish to any BBQ to beautify the buffet.

PREP + COOK TIME 10 MINUTES **SERVES** 8

4 cups shredded green cabbage

1 cup shredded red cabbage

½ cup vegan mayo

2 tablespoons chopped fresh or dried dill

1 teaspoon rice vinegar

1½ tablespoons pure maple syrup

½ teaspoon salt

½ teaspoon freshly ground black pepper

Put all the ingredients in a large bowl, mix with tongs, and serve.

x GF

x SF (if you use soy-free vegan mayo)

x NF

DREAMY SOUPS + STEWS

that are healing

CREAMY DREAMY
Broccoli Soup

I thought my love affair with creamy soup was over, but I was wrong. There are so many products on the market that replace cream now, making it easier than ever to make the creamy soups you love cream-less. Broccoli is truly a super vegetable and one of the healthiest foods on the planet. It is anti-cancerous and full of vitamins and minerals. Enjoy a soup that is good . . . both for your soul and your body.

SERVES 4 **TOTAL PREP TIME** TOTAL PREP TIME: 30 MINUTES

4 large (1 pound) heads broccoli, chopped
⅓ cup chopped onion
1½ teaspoons salt
2 cups water
2 cups coconut milk creamer (I use the unflavored coconut coffee creamer)
½ teaspoon freshly ground black pepper

X **GF**
X **SF**
X **NF**

Put the broccoli in a large soup pot, along with the onion, salt, and water. Bring to a boil over medium-high heat, and cook until the broccoli is tender, then stir in the coconut cream. Remove the pot from the heat. Let the soup cool slightly, then use a blender stick or blender to purée it until smooth.

Recipe Notes:
I love this soup with French bread or a warm flour tortilla. I am sure no one would kick you out of bed for topping it with crackers. Sweet dreams! Broccoli is a great source of vitamins K and C, a good source of folate (folic acid), and a source of potassium and fiber. Vitamin C builds collagen, which forms body tissue and bone and helps cuts and wounds heal, and it's also a powerful antioxidant that protects the body from damaging free radicals.

PERFECT POTATO
Leek Soup

I am a huge fan of potatoes—all kinds of potatoes—and pretty much any recipe that has potatoes in it. This is my remake of traditional potato leek soup, and it satisfies all kinds of eaters, even the picky ones. Serve it with warm French bread, vegan butter, a side salad, and call it a meal. Leeks are in the onion family and add so much flavor to this soup. I like the soup puréed, but if you prefer it chunky, just don't purée it as much.

PREP + COOK TIME 30 MINUTES **SERVES** 8

1 teaspoon olive oil

⅔ cup chopped onion

¼ cup sliced leeks

4 cups water

4 pounds golden potatoes (skin on), chopped into ½-inch cubes

4 cups almond milk

1 tablespoon salt

Freshly ground black pepper

Heat the olive oil in a large soup pot over medium heat. Add the onion and leeks, and cook until golden. Add the water and potatoes, bring the liquid to a boil, and cook covered for about 10 to 15 minutes or until the potatoes are falling apart. Strain out half the water. Add the almond milk and salt. Cook for 10 to 15 more minutes, then take the pot off the heat and let the soup cool for 20 minutes. Use a blender stick or blender to purée the soup to your preferred consistency.

Recipe Notes:

Potatoes are low in calories and have no fat. Eating a potato with the skin will make you feel fuller longer than carbohydrates made with refined flour—like white rice and pasta—do, because the starch in a potato digests more slowly than refined carbohydrates.

On leeks, cut off the root and leaves, about a ¼ higher than them. Then cut lengthwise to where it starts to feel fibrous and then harder to cut. Then chop what's remaining as you would an onion. If its hard to slice it will be hard to eat.

x **GF**

x **SF**

x **NF (if you use hemp, coconut, or seed milk instead of almond milk)**

EATING WELL
IS A
FORM OF
self respect

I LOVE A RAINY NIGHT
Lentil Stew

This is called a stew for a reason, and it is in no way, shape, or form a soup, because it is thick and hearty and serves as a meal. Serve it with a salad on the side, and it will probably become one of your favorite go-to dinners. For an even heartier meal, serve it over brown rice.

PREP + COOK TIME 30 MINUTES **SERVES** 8

- 2 tablespoons olive oil
- 1 celery rib, chopped
- 1 yellow onion, chopped
- 2 teaspoons minced garlic
- 2 medium carrots, peeled and sliced into half moons
- 2 cups chopped unpeeled potatoes (½-inch pieces)
- 4 cups water, divided
- 1¼ cups dried lentils
- 2 teaspoons salt

Heat the olive oil in a large soup pot over low heat. Add the celery, onion, and garlic. Cook for about 5 minutes, stirring a few times. Add the carrots, potatoes, and 3 cups of the water. Bring to a simmer, then add the lentils and salt. Cover and cook for 30 to 40 minutes, stirring every 10 minutes. When the lentils are tender, add the last cup of water and simmer uncovered for 10 minutes. Serve warm.

Recipe Notes:

Lentils are little powerhouses of nutrition! Eat lentils and reap their health benefits, including lower cholesterol, a healthier heart, better digestive health, stabilized blood sugar, good protein, and weight loss. Lentils help to reduce blood cholesterol, since they contain high levels of soluble fiber.

x GF
x SF
x NF

WELCOME HOME
Pumpkin Soup

I believe pumpkin should be eaten all year long. It is all sorts of good for you. This recipe was on the menu when I first bought the café. We have changed it a little, but it is still original. This was always a favorite of our guests at the café.

PREP + COOK TIME 30 MINUTES **SERVES** 8

1 teaspoon olive oil

½ cup chopped onion

2 tablespoons chopped garlic

2 tablespoons chopped fresh ginger

1 tablespoon salt

½ cup white wine

½ bunch kale, stemmed and chopped

1 teaspoon curry powder

½ teaspoon red pepper flakes

2 (15-ounce) cans pumpkin pureé

4 cups water

2 (15-ounce) cans coconut milk

Toasted Pumpkin Seeds (recipe follows), for serving

X **GF**

X **SF**

X **NF**

Heat the olive oil in a large soup pot over medium-high heat. Add the onion, garlic, and ginger and sauté until translucent, then add the salt, wine, kale, curry powder, and pepper flakes. Cook, stirring, until the kale starts to wilt. Add the pumpkin, water, and coconut milk, constantly stirring so the kale does not stick. Cook for about 30 minutes. Ladle the soup into individual bowls, and serve topped with pumpkin seeds (recipe follows).

Toasted Pumpkin Seeds

MAKES 1 CUP

1 cup raw pumpkin seeds
1 teaspoon olive oil
1 teaspoon salt

Preheat the oven to 400°F, and line a baking sheet with parchment.

In a medium bowl, toss the pumpkin seeds with the oil and salt. Transfer the seeds to the prepared baking sheet, and bake for 12 to 15 minutes, or until they turn golden brown. Keep an eye on them as you bake, because these will turn from done to overdone quickly.

Recipe Notes:
Pumpkin's orange color is a big clue that it is loaded with the antioxidant beta-carotene, which is one of the plant carotenoids that is converted to Vitamin A in the body. Vitamin A is essential for strong eyesight, a healthy immune system, and glowing skin.

TAKE ME TO FUNGI TOWN

Mushroom Soup

I could literally eat this soup all day. It is so tasty that even people who do not like mushrooms like it. The secret is using a cashew cheese base, which rivals all real cream counterparts. It has a light texture but is super filling. Use any mushrooms you like, but I love button mushrooms, so that is what you'll find in this recipe.

PREP + COOK TIME 30 MINUTES **SERVES** 6

1 teaspoon olive oil
½ cup chopped onion
1½ pounds button mushrooms, quartered
3 cups water
1½ cups cashews
2 teaspoons salt

Heat the olive oil in a soup

On medium heat add all ingredients into a large soup pot. Cook for 15 minutes on a rolling boil stirring occasionally until mushrooms are soft. Remove from heat, let it cool slightly, then purée the soup either with a blender stick or in a blender. Serve warm.

Recipe Notes:
Many mushrooms are also good sources of selenium, an antioxidant mineral, as well as copper, niacin, potassium, and phosphorous. Additionally, mushrooms provide protein, vitamin C, and iron.

X **GF**

APPIES
+ SNACKS
Small healthy starters

RAW AND ROASTED
Veggie Tray

People, out of the goodness of their hearts, are always buying me vegetable trays from Costco, because they do not know what to feed me. I honestly started disliking them in a big way. So, for parties, I started to bring my own to show people how fun vegetables can be. This is a mix of raw and roasted.

PREP + COOK TIME 20 MINUTES **SERVES** 6

½ **pound green beans, trimmed**

8 **mini bell peppers**

2 **carrots, peeled and cut into sticks**

2 **celery ribs, cut into sticks**

½ **head cauliflower, cut into bite-size pieces**

½ **large head broccoli, cut into bite-size pieces**

½ **teaspoon olive oil**

1 **teaspoon salt**

Kale, for garnish

Hummus (page 139) and Paniolo Ranch Dressing (page 191), for serving

x **GF**

x **SF**

x **NF**

Preheat the oven to 400°F. Put the green beans and bell peppers on a baking sheet, drizzle with olive oil, and season with salt. Roast for 10 minutes, until they are tender-crisp.

Spread a few kale leaves on a serving platter, then arrange the vegetables on top, each in their own section, and nestle in bowls of hummus and ranch.

HAPPY
Hummus

It's a hummus that makes everyone happy. This recipe is half peanuts and half garbanzo beans, believe it or not, and it is a crowd pleaser. Peanuts are actually legumes, so it is no wonder that peanut butter goes so good with beans. Serve this with fresh veggies, tortilla chips, or in a wrap.

MAKES 1½ CUPS **PREP TIME** 10 MINUTES

3 garlic cloves, peeled
**½ cup packed fresh cilantro
leaves**
**1 (15-ounce) can garbanzo
beans, drained
and rinsed**
1 tablespoon olive oil
**3 tablespoons smooth
peanut butter**
**2 tablespoons freshly
squeezed lemon juice
(from 1 to 2 lemons),
or to taste**
½ teaspoon salt

Finely chop the garlic and cilantro in a food processor. Add the beans, oil, salt, and peanut butter, and then half of the lemon juice. Process until the beans are puréed, stopping midway to scrape the sides of the processor bowl. Taste and add more lemon juice as desired. Serve immediately, or cover and refrigerate for up to three days.

Recipe Notes:
If you have peanut allergy, use tahini instead of peanut butter.

x **GF (if served with gluten-free
bread or crackers)**
x **SF**
x **NF (if you use tahini instead of
peanut butter)**

TAKE 2
Artichoke Dip

A play on the cheesy, creamy original! This is so decadent, and in all the right ways. It is so easy, yet brings more compliments than any other dish I make. Artichokes pretty much top the superfood chart for antioxidants and fiber. Do not let the great taste of artichokes make you forget how nutritious they are!

SERVES 4 **TOTAL PREP TIME** 35 MINUTES

2 cups canned artichokes hearts chopped

½ can (2 ounces) diced green chilies

½ cup vegan mayo

½ cup shredded vegan mozzarella cheese

½ teaspoon salt

Crackers or bread, for serving

Preheat the oven to 350°F. In a medium bowl, mix together the artichoke hearts, chilies, mayo, cheese, and salt. Scrape the mixture into an oven-safe dish and bake for 30 minutes or until bubbly and starting to brown on top. Serve warm with crackers or bread.

X GF (served with gluten-free bread or crackers)
X SF (if you use soy-free vegan mayo and cheese)
X NF

TOMATO LOVE
Bruschetta

I am not the biggest fan of tomatoes on their own, but I am quite fond of them in recipes. This is a delicious way to showcase tomatoes from the garden. Ancient Bread (see page 183) pairs perfectly with the bruschetta topping—food in its simplest form. These are great as an appetizer, light lunch, or dinner.

SERVES 6 **PREP TIME** 10 MINUTES

1 recipe Ancient Bread (page 183) or 1 French bread loaf, sliced

2 pounds tomatoes, finely diced

½ cup fresh basil leaves, cut into long, thin strips

2 tablespoons minced garlic

1 teaspoon salt

Lettuce leaves, for garnish

balsamic vinegar drizzle

Toast your bread slices lightly in the oven.

In a large bowl, mix together the tomatoes, basil, garlic, and salt. Set aside. Cover a serving plate with the lettuce leaves, cover with a layer of toast, and top with the bruschetta. I love topping it with a little balsamic as well. Serve and enjoy.

Recipe Notes:
Tomatoes are the major dietary source of the antioxidant lycopene, which has been linked to many health benefits, including reduced risk of heart disease and cancer.

x GF (if you use gluten-free bread)
x SF
x NF

YOU'RE NOT NAUGHTY
Nachos

Who doesn't crave nachos? Crispy, crunchy, salty, and creamy. Just because you are trying to eat healthier doesn't mean you have to miss out on nachos. Play around with toppings you love, and spice it up with some hot sauce, if you like.

PREP + COOK TIME 20 MINUTES **SERVES** 6

¾ **cup canned black beans,
   drained and
   rinsed Salt**
**5 cups restaurant style
   tortilla chips**
¾ **cup shredded vegan
   mozzarella or cheddar cheese**
¾ **cup diced tomatoes**
1 ripe avocado, chopped
**1 can (2½ ounces) sliced
   olives**
½ **red onion, sliced**
**1 packet (1 oz) enchilada
   seasoning**
**1 container (8 oz) vegan
   sour cream**
**2 tablespoons chopped
   fresh cilantro**

x **GF**
x **SF**
x **NF**

Preheat the oven to 400°F.
Heat up the black beans in a small saucepan, and season with a little sea salt.

Arrange the chips on platter baking sheet or large baking dish, and sprinkle with the beans, cheese, tomatoes, avocado, olives, and onion. Bake for 15 minutes, until cheese is melted.

While is the nachos are baking, put the enchilada seasoning in a small bowl, add 2 tablespoons hot water, and mix with a fork. Stir this into the container of sour cream.

Remove the nachos from the oven and top with the seasoned sour cream and cilantro. Enjoy immediately.

SALTY OLIVE
Tapenade

This is like a salty bruschetta. It is delicious on top of toast, crackers, salads, and sandwiches, or as a garnish on any dish. This recipe can be prepared ahead of time and lasts in the fridge for months.

PREP + COOK TIME 10 MINUTES **MAKES** 2 CUPS

2 garlic cloves

⅓ cup olive oil

1½ cups pitted Kalamata olives

2 tablespoons capers, drained

2 tablespoons Italian parsley

½ teaspoon salt

Pulse the garlic in a food processor until finely chopped. Add the rest of the ingredients and process for about 30 seconds. The mixture should be very finely chopped with some texture. Store the tapenade in a covered glass bowl in the fridge for up to two weeks.

x GF

x SF

x NF

STUFFED-UP
Mushrooms

Mushrooms are amazing and versatile. As a vegetable, they have a meaty texture that is filling and satisfying. Most stuffed mushrooms are filled with fatty ingredients and other yucky things. These are gluten-free and cheese-less, but you will never know.

PREP + COOK TIME 15 MINUTES **SERVES** 4
(APPROXIMATELY 16 MUSHROOMS)

1 (24-ounce) package button mushrooms

1 carrot, peeled and chopped

1 celery rib, chopped

¼ small onion minced

½ cup gluten-free crackers

1 teaspoon olive oil

3 tablespoons Paniolo Ranch Dressing (see page 191) or vegan mayo

1 teaspoon salt

Preheat the oven to 350°F.

Stem the mushroom (reserving the stems), and put the caps on a baking sheet. Combine the mushroom stems, carrot, and celery in a food processor, and pulse until finely chopped. In a food processor or blender, or by hand, crush the gluten-free crackers.

Heat the oil in a medium skillet over medium heat. Add the minced vegetables and cook for 3 minutes, then add the cracker crumbs, dressing, and salt. Cook for another 3 minutes, stirring constantly, until browned on top. Remove the skillet from the heat and let it cool, then spoon the filling into the mushroom caps (about 1 tablespoon per cap). Bake the stuffed mushrooms for 15 minutes, until golden brown and crunchy on the top.

x **GF**

x **SF (if you use soy-free vegan mayo)**

x **NF**

MAIN
MEALS
Dinner is served

SHORTCUT

lasagna

This recipe reminds me of vegetarian lasagna. The tofu crumbles mixed with cashew cheese really resemble ricotta and mozzarella. I only add spinach to mine because I prefer it simple; however, you can add whatever veggies you like. I use gluten-free brown rice noodles.

PREP + COOK TIME 70 MINUTES **SERVES** 6

2 (16-ounce) packages medium to firm tofu, crumbled by hand

2 teaspoons salt

1 recipe Cashew Cheese (see page 198)

2 jars (25 ounces) tomato sauce

1 package (10 ounce) uncooked gluten-free lasagna noodles

½ onion, chopped

1 (16-ounce) package fresh spinach (You can also use frozen spinach; just thaw it completely and squeeze out as much water as possible.)

Preheat the oven to 375°F.

x **GF**

x **NF (if you replace the cashew cheese with nut-free vegan cheese)**

x **SF (if you replace the tofu with cauliflower crumbles)**

Put the crumbled tofu in a medium bowl, add the salt and cashew cheese, and mix well.

In a 10 x 15-inch glass baking dish, start assembling the lasagna: Spread ½ cup tomato sauce in the bottom of the dish, then top with a layer of noodles (I do not cook mine beforehand), another ½ cup tomato sauce, half the onion, 1 cup tofu crumbles, 1½ cups spinach, and another layer of noodles. Repeat one more time—½ cup tomato sauce, onion, tofu, spinach, and noodles—and top with the rest of the tomato sauce, making sure to spread it evenly over the noodles so they will cook. Cover with foil and bake for 40 minutes or until sauce is bubbly. Remove the lasagna from the oven, let it cool slightly, and cut into six pieces. Serve hot with Caesar salad (page 110).

You will have tomato sauce left over, but I like to use mine to garnish the plate.

These are my spin on fish tacos. They are crunchy, fresh, and perfect for warm weather, and taste creamy with every delicious bite. I use ripe avocados dipped in breadcrumbs and bake them until they are crispy and slice them length-wise to resemble fish sticks. I combine them with slow-cooked black beans and add both to either flour or corn tortillas. These are a real crowd pleaser and a favorite family meal. I guarantee you will win over everyone with this recipe.

HEAVENLY FRIED AVOCADO
Tacos

SERVES 6 **PREP TIME** 30 MINUTES

- **1 box gluten-free breadcrumbs (10.5 ounces) (make sure it is vegan)**
- **1 teaspoon salt, divided**
- **2 ripe avocados, peeled and sliced**
- **1 tablespoon olive oil, plus more for frying**
- **3 teaspoons relish**
- **1 cup vegan mayo**
- **1 head green cabbage, shredded**
- **¼ cup shredded red cabbage**
- **12 tortillas (gluten-free flour or corn, your choice)**
- **Hot sauce (optional)**

x **GF (if you use corn tortillas)**
x **SF (if you use soy-free vegan mayo)**
x **NF**

Preheat the oven to 400°F (if baking the avocado).
Put the breadcrumbs in a shallow bowl and mix in ½ teaspoon of the salt. Dip the avocado slices into the breadcrumbs, pressing to coat; set aside.

You can either pan fry or bake the avocado. To pan fry: coat a large skillet with oil and place it over medium heat. When the oil is hot, add the breaded avocado slices and cook for 4 minutes per side, or until golden brown. Transfer to a paper towel–lined plate to drain. To bake: line a baking sheet with parchment and grease the parchment with a little olive oil. Arrange the avocado slices on top and bake for 15 minutes or until golden.

To make the sauce, combine the relish, remaining ½ teaspoon salt, and vegan mayo in a small bowl. Stir well with a fork until no lumps remain. Taste and add a little relish juice for extra flavor.

Heat the tortillas in a skillet over low heat, or warm them in the oven.

Mix together the green and red cabbage in a large bowl.

In the center of each tortilla, place 2 avocado nuggets, a handful of cabbage, a dollop of sauce, and a few drops of hot sauce, if you like. Celebrate this miracle on Taco Tuesday or Sacred Sunday.

CURRY IN A
Hurry

This is our version of East Indian cauliflower curry—light in color and more saucy than brothy, a quick dish to enjoy at your leisure. Served over basmati rice, this dish feels healing.

SERVES 4 **TOTAL PREP TIME** 20 MINUTES

1 tablespoon olive oil

¼ cup chopped onion

½ head cauliflower chopped into ½-inch pieces

2 small gold potatoes, peeled and cut into 1-inch pieces

1 carrot, peeled and sliced

½ cup water

2 teaspoons ground turmeric

1 teaspoon ground coriander

1 teaspoon ground cumin

1 teaspoon salt

1 (13.5-ounce) can full-fat coconut milk

Cooked basmati rice, for serving

Combine the oil and onion in a soup pot over medium heat. Cook for 1 minute, then add the cauliflower, potatoes, carrot, and water. Cover and cook until the vegetables are tender, about 10 minutes. Stir in the turmeric, coriander, cumin, and salt. Mix until everything is coated, then pour in the coconut milk. Let the curry simmer for a few minutes to marry the flavors, and serve hot over basmati rice.

Recipe Notes:

Did you know that cauliflower is one of the healthiest foods in the world? It helps just about every part of your body, so do your own research and you will want to eat it every day like I do!

X **GF**

X **SF**

X **NF**

I always loved eggplant parmesan. The salty, crispy eggplant baked with tomato sauce and cheese is one of my favorite meals. When I changed the original recipe to make it vegan and gluten-free, I knew I had a keeper.

EGGPLANT
No Parm

PREP + COOK TIME 20 MINUTES **SERVES** 6

1 package crackers, 4 bread slices, or 1 cup store-bought breadcrumbs (I use gluten free)

½ cup brown rice flour

1½ teaspoons salt

½ cup nondairy milk

2 pounds eggplant, cut into ⅛-inch-thick rounds or horizontal slices

4 tablespoons olive oil

2 cups Cashew Cheese (see page 198)

1 jar (25 ounces) store-bought tomato sauce

x GF
x SF
x NF (instead of cashew cheese use store-bought nut-free cheese)

Preheat the oven to 400°F.

In a food processor, process bread or crackers into crumbs (omit this step if you are using store-bought breadcrumbs). Transfer the breadcrumbs to a shallow bowl or plate. In a shallow bowl, mix together the brown rice flour and salt. Pour the milk into another shallow bowl.

Dip the eggplant slices into the flour, then the milk, and finally the breadcrumbs, pressing to coat them on both sides.

Lightly coat a baking sheet with 2 tablespoons of the olive oil. Place the breaded eggplant on the baking sheet and drizzle with the remaining 2 tablespoons of olive oil. Bake for 30 minutes, until the eggplant is golden. Heat the tomato sauce in a saucepan over medium heat.

Recipe Notes:

Once the eggplant is baked, there are two ways to proceed:

- **Stack the ingredients in individual bowls (tomato sauce, eggplant, and cashew cream; repeat) and serve immediately.**

- **Assemble and bake: Spread a thin layer of tomato sauce in the bottom of a 9 x 13-inch baking dish, top with a layer of eggplant, then cashew cream, and repeat twice more, finishing with a layer of tomato sauce and cashew cheese. Bake at 350°F for 30 minutes, until crust has started to turn golden brown. I enjoy it both ways, and I always serve this with sautéed kale and rice on the side.**

MATCH MADE IN HEAVEN

Coconut Mac Nut Tofu

PREP + COOK TIME 1 HOUR **MAKES** 4

COCONUT CREAM SAUCE

- ¼ cup grated fresh ginger
- ¼ cup minced garlic
- 1 tablespoon olive oil
- 1 cup white wine (optional)
- 1½ tablespoons salt
- Pinch of curry powder
- Pinch of ground cumin
- 3 (13.5-ounce) cans full-fat coconut milk

COCONUT MAC NUT CRUST

- 1½ cups macadamia nuts, chopped and toasted
- 4 cups unsweetened shredded coconut
- 1½ cups brown rice flour
- 2 tablespoons grated fresh ginger
- 2 tablespoons minced garlic
- 2 tablespoons salt

TOFU

- 2 (16-ounce) packages firm tofu, drained and cut into ¼ inch rectangular slices

Preheat the oven to 350°F.

To make the coconut cream sauce: In a medium saucepan, sauté the ginger and garlic with the olive oil until golden. Add the wine (if using), salt, curry powder, and cumin. Cook for 4 minutes, then pour in the coconut milk. Reduce the heat to medium-low and cook for 30 minutes or until the sauce thickens. Remove from the heat and set aside to cool.

To make the coconut mac nut crust: Mix all the ingredients together in a bowl. Set aside. This is good on everything. I call it my vegan parm. (It will keep in an airtight container in the fridge for up to a month).

To bake the tofu: Arrange the tofu slices in a baking dish in a single layer. Pour a little coconut cream over the tofu, then sprinkle with the nut crust. Bake for 25 minutes, until the crust is toasted.

Recipe Notes:

I serve the tofu on mashed purple sweet potatoes (follow the Dreamy Mashed Potato recipe on page 175) with roasted green beans and ½ cup coconut cream sauce.

x GF

This was our signature dish at my café. It is a great way to get your family to fall in love with tofu. The combination of coconut, macadamia nuts, and tofu is heavenly!

BBQ SAUCED
Cauliflower

BBQ cauliflower is one of my and my family's favorite recipes. We serve it with mashed potatoes and sautéed greens for a perfect balance of color and flavor on the plate. Keep leftovers in the fridge to enjoy as a finger snack all week.

SERVES 4 **PREP TIME** 45 MINUTES

1 large head cauliflower,
chopped into 1-inch pieces

¼ red onion, chopped

2 tablespoons olive oil

3 tablespoons tamari

3 tablespoons chopped
fresh or dried dill

1 ½ cups No BBQ Needed
Sauce (see page 200, or
your favorite jarred BBQ
sauce)

x **GF**

x **SF**

x **NF**

Preheat the oven to 400°F.

In a large bowl, toss together the cauliflower, onion, olive oil, tamari, and dill, then transfer the mixture to a 9 x 13-inch glass baking dish. Roast for 30 minutes, remove from the oven, and coat in the BBQ sauce.

Recipe Notes:

If you don't like cauliflower, use tofu.

Opposite page, served with Dreamy
Mashed Potato and chopped kale

MOM'S HOMESTYLE
Chili

My mom was not a big eater, but with six kids, she had to cook. Her recipes were simple and easy, and we all loved them. This recipe is super easy and quick to make. It uses canned beans and tomatoes, which I always keep in the pantry for last-minute meals. When I changed my diet to organic, this recipe was out because they did not have an organic equivalent. It was life-changing when organic renditions of my favorite bean blends became available.

PREP + COOK TIME 1 HOUR **SERVES** 6-8

2 (15-ounce) cans chili beans
2 (15-ounce) cans baked beans
1 (15-ounce) can kidney beans,
   drained and rinsed
1 (15-ounce) can stewed tomatoes,
   drained
1 teaspoon chili powder
½ teaspoon salt

In a large pot over medium heat, combine all the ingredients. In

In a large pot on medium heat, mix all ingredients together and bring to a low boil (this will take about 10 minutes), then reduce the heat to low and cook for 45 minutes, stirring occasionally. Take off the heat, and serve hot.

Recipe Notes:
I always have toppings of vegan cheese, chopped onions, and vegan sour cream on the side. It is delicious with brown rice or French bread with vegan butter. Thanks, Mom!

x **GF**
x **SF**
x **NF**

YOU MANGO
ME CRAZY
Pizza

This is a fun ode to Hawaiian pizza—creamy, sweet, and savory. The dough is crisp and chewy, and you can choose gluten-free or not. I included my favorite pizza variations below, but I want you to have fun with this and make your own masterpiece!

SERVES 6 **PREP TIME** 10 MINUTES

½ recipe My Heart Pizza
   Dough (see page 186)
½ recipe Coconut Cream Sauce
   (see Coconut Mac Nut Tofu,
   page 160)
1 bunch kale, stemmed and
   chopped into 1-inch pieces
1 cup chopped mango
   (bite-size pieces)
½ cup macadamia nuts,
   chopped

Preheat the oven to 475°F.

On each round of dough, spread the cream sauce as you would pizza sauce. Next, add a layer of kale (about a handful), followed by the mango and macadamia nuts. Bake for 10 to 12 minutes or until dough is golden brown and sauce starts to thicken. Remove from the oven and let cool before slicing.

Variations:

Tomato sauce, artichoke hearts, olives, sun-dried tomatoes, and roasted bell peppers.
BBQ sauce, vegan mozzarella cheese, onions, pineapple, and spinach.

x **SF**
x **GF if using Gluten-Free dough**
x **NF if you omit the nuts**

MAC AND CHEESE
Yes please!

Yes, please, to mac and cheese—but double yes, please without the dairy and gluten! Have fun and add scrumptious sautéed vegetables or top with breadcrumbs. I use carrots with cashew cheese to create the sauce.

PREP + COOK TIME 20 MINUTES **SERVES** 6

1 package (16 ounces) brown rice elbow macaroni

1 carrot, peeled and thinly sliced

2 cups Cashew Cheese (see page 198)

1 teaspoon salt

Freshly ground black pepper

Hot sauce (optional)

x **GF**

Cook the pasta according to the box instructions, then drain.

In a small pot of water, boil or steam the carrots for about 10 minutes or until they are soft. Remove them from the heat, and drain.

In a blender, combine the carrots and cashew cheese; blend until smooth.

Add the cooked pasta back to the pot, and stir in the cashew cheese mixture and salt. Taste and season with black pepper and hot sauce as desired.

SIDES
+ TASTES
Pretty up your plate

THE ROAST OF
Cauliflower

It is no secret how much I love cauliflower. And, at 20 calories per cup, you should love it, too. This recipe is a staple in my house. A lot of times when I make it, my kids eat it all before it even makes it to the dinner table.

PREP + COOK TIME 35 MINUTES **SERVES** 4

1 head cauliflower, cut
   into 1-inch florets
2 teaspoons olive oil
1½ teaspoons salt

Preheat the oven to 400°F.

Place the cauliflower in a 9 x 13-inch glass baking dish, drizzle with the olive oil, and sprinkle with the salt. Stir it so that all your pieces are coated. Roast for about 30 minutes, until the cauliflower starts to brown and caramelize. Let it cool before serving. Good luck getting it to the table!

Recipe Notes:
- As you can see in the photo, this recipe is versatile. You can swap out cauliflower for almost any vegetable. Try carrots, Brussels sprouts, asparagus, or any of your other favorites.
- Just 1 cup of cauliflower contains 77 percent of the recommended daily value of vitamin C. It's also a good source of vitamin K, protein, thiamin, riboflavin, niacin, magnesium, phosphorus, fiber, vitamin B6, folate, pantothenic acid, potassium, and manganese.

x GF
x SF
x NF

SWEET POTATO
Nuggets of Love

Sweet potatoes. The superfood of potatoes! They are sweet, savory, and hearty. As a vegan, I've fallen even more in love with them. I enjoy these nuggets for breakfast, as croutons on a salad, as a dinner side, and straight out of the fridge as leftovers, sometimes all from the same batch. It is a weekly staple at my house. In this recipe, I use purple sweet potatoes, but you can use any variety you like.

SERVES 4 **PREP TIME** 45 MINUTES

4 pounds purple sweet potatoes, cut into cubes, fries, or nuggets (I leave the skin on)

2 tablespoons olive oil

2 teaspoons salt

Preheat the oven to 450°F. Line a baking sheet with parchment.

In a bowl, toss the sweet potato nuggets with the olive oil and salt, then transfer them to the prepared baking sheet and spread them out in a single layer. Roast for 30 to 40 minutes. At the 20-minute mark, use a spatula to carefully flip the potatoes to ensure even cooking. They are done when they're golden brown and soft all the way through. Remove from the oven, let cool slightly, and serve.

Recipe Notes:

Sweet potatoes of all varieties are high in vitamin A, vitamin C, and manganese. They are also a good source of copper, dietary fiber, vitamin B6, potassium, and iron.

X **GF**
X **SF**
X **NF**

BEAUTY
and the Beets

I love roasted veggies, as you will notice on the next few pages. Roasting brings out a caramelized flavor in vegetables. I love roasting beets because it allows me to keep the skin on and save time by not peeling. Eat these instead of chips as a snack, or throw them on a salad.

SERVES 4 **TOTAL PREP TIME** 35 MINUTES

2 pounds beets, cut into ½-inch cubes (skin left on)
2 teaspoons olive oil
1 teaspoon salt

Preheat the oven to 400°F. Line a baking sheet with parchment.

In a large bowl, toss the beets with the olive oil and salt, then transfer to the baking sheet and spread the beets out in a single layer. Roast for 25 minutes, until tender. Store in an airtight container in the fridge for up to four days.

Recipe Notes:
Beets are a wonderful weight-loss food! They contain essential vitamins and minerals, including magnesium, potassium, vitamin c, and iron, that boost immunity. Beets also help to flush water from the system to effectively prevent and reduce water retention, which often causes excess weight.

X **GF**
X **SF**
X **NF**

DREAMY
Mashed Potatoes

I love mashed potatoes—and not just at the holidays. They make the perfect bed for whatever savory dish you are serving.

SERVES 6 **PREP TIME** 25 MINUTES

8 cups water

6 russet potatoes, peeled and quartered

¼ cup vegan butter

1 teaspoon salt

½ to ¾ cup nondairy milk or creamer (unsweetened and unflavored), divided

Bring the water to a boil in a large pot over medium-high heat. Add the potatoes, and cook until they are soft but not falling apart, about 20 minutes.

Drain the potatoes and return them to the pot. Add the butter, salt, and ½ cup of the milk. Mash with a potato masher until all the lumps are gone. If desired, stir in another ¼ cup of milk.

Recipe Notes:

Sub russet potatoes with sweet potatoes or cauliflower, and follow the same instructions.

x **GF**

x **SF (if the vegan butter is soy free)**

x **NF (if the non-dairy milk is hemp, coconut, or seed milk)**

ROASTED PUMPKIN
Winter Squash All Year

Have you ever had roasted pumpkin? I think it's better than pumpkin pie. It is sweet and caramel rich. It makes a fabulous side dish and is surprisingly tasty as a salad topping. I use kabocha pumpkin because it grows locally here in Kauai. You also can substitute pumpkin for winter squash. I always recommend local and fresh, wherever you may be.

PREP + COOK TIME 35 TO 45 MINUTES **SERVES** 6

1 (5 pound) pumpkin, seeds scooped out and saved for later, flesh cut into 1-inch pieces (skin left on)
3 tablespoons olive oil
2 teaspoons salt

Preheat the oven to 400°F. Line a baking sheet with parchment.

In a large bowl, toss the pumpkin with the olive oil and salt. Transfer to the baking sheet, and spread the pumpkin in a single layer. Roast for 35 to 45 minutes, until golden brown spots appear.

Recipe Notes:

- **Pumpkin is not just for fall anymore. The energy-boosting benefits alone are enough reason to eat this veggie all year round!**
- **Save the seeds and roast them with salt and pepper.**
- **Eating pumpkin is good for the heart. The fiber, potassium, and vitamin C content in pumpkin all support heart health. Studies suggest that consuming enough potassium may be almost as important as decreasing sodium intake for the treatment of hypertension (high blood pressure).**

x GF
x SF
x NF

ANCIENT BREAD
(Pain in My à l'Ancienne)

MAKES 2 LARGE LOAVES OR 4 SMALLER ROUNDS
TOTAL PREP TIME 40 MINUTES, PLUS OVERNIGHT REST TIME

4½ cups all-purpose flour, plus more as needed

2 teaspoons salt

1½ teaspoons active dry yeast

3 cups water, plus more as needed

Combine the flour, salt, and yeast in the bowl of an electric mixer fitted with the paddle attachment. Turn the mixer to low speed, and stream in the water, a little at a time, until the mixture starts to get sticky and doughy. Bring the mixer up to medium for about 30 seconds. Sprinkle a little flour (about ¼ cup) over the top and underneath the dough. Transfer the dough to a large bowl, cover with plastic wrap, and refrigerate overnight. The next day, preheat the oven to 450°F. Transfer the dough to a floured surface and divide it into 2 to 4 pieces (depending on whether you want two loaves or four rounds). Form the pieces into loaves or rounds, coat with a little flour, and arrange them on a baking sheet. Bake for 15 to 20 minutes, until golden brown.

Recipe Notes:

- **If you don't have the time for an overnight rise, add 1 extra teaspoon of yeast to the dough, and let it rise on the counter for 1 hour instead of in the fridge overnight.**
- **I use this for anything from bruschetta, to sandwich bread, to French toast, to croutons, and of course, as just fresh bread at the table. This bread is versatile—perfect to use with any meal.**
- **To make it gluten free, replace the flour with brown rice flour and add one tablespoon xanthan gum. Coat with brown rice flour.**

x GF

x SF (if using brown rice flour)

x NF

Pain a l'ancienne is an old-fashioned bread that is not so easy to make, but well worth the effort. This recipe is from a time when we made our own bread, before there were stores. It is a cold-yeasted bread, meaning that the recipe calls for cold water, allowing it to rise on its own, whereas warm water and sugar speed up the process. I love this dough, because it can be made ahead of time, and it's very versatile. This bread is a great example of why simple is better. There are very few ingredients, and although there is some time and effort involved, the taste itself is worth the wait.

PIZZA MY
Heart Dough

MAKES ENOUGH FOR 6 MEDIUM (8") PIZZAS
TOTAL PREP TIME: 25 MINUTES, PLUS 30 MINUTES RISING TIME

4 cups warm water

2 packets (¼ ounce size) active dry yeast (4½ teaspoons)

1 tablespoon sugar, pure maple syrup, or agave nectar

9 cups all-purpose flour, plus more as needed

2 tablespoons salt

Olive oil

x GF (if you use brown rice flour)
x SF
x NF

In a bowl or large measuring cup, mix together the warm water, yeast, and sugar. Set aside for about 10 minutes, until the mixture is foamy.

In the meantime, in the bowl of an electric mixer fitted with the paddle attachment, combine the flour and salt. Add the yeast mixture and start mixing on low; as the dough begins to come together, slowly increase the speed to medium. When it resembles dough, turn it off. (If you'd rather mix the dough by hand, follow the same instructions, but be ready for a lot of mixing!)

Grab another large bowl, and coat it lightly with olive oil. Dust your dough with a little flour, and transfer it to the oiled bowl. Cover with plastic wrap or a dish towel, and let it rise at room temperature for about 30 minutes, until the dough has doubled in size.

When the dough is finished rising, punch it down, literally. Flour a surface and transfer your dough to it. Cut the dough into 6 fairly even pieces. Roll the 6 pieces into 8-inch-diameter disc, cover, and let rise again for 20 minutes. Transfer the dough discs to a lightly floured baking sheet, and slowly stretch them to your desired pizza size.
You can premake to this point and wrap each individually in plastic wrap and freeze them for up to two months.

When I make dough, I make a lot so I can freeze it and have it on hand for a while. This dough can be used for pizza, cinnamon rolls, focaccia, breadsticks … the possibilities go on and on. It is chewy and light and crispy all at once.

Recipe Notes:

- Top this dough as you like, and bake at 475°F for 10 minutes. See page 167 for topping ideas.
- If you are making focaccia or cinnamon rolls, follow the directions in that recipe for shaping and baking temps and times.
- For gluten-free pizza dough, replace the flour with brown rice flour and 1½ tablespoons xanthan gum. Follow the directions as written above; however, you should shape the dough on the sheet pan, as it can fall apart when transferring over.

DRESSINGS
+ SAUCES

It's all in the sauce

HERB
Oil

This oil will add that extra something to any savory recipe. I love it drizzled on avocado toast or pasta, or as a dressing for a Greek-style salad.

PREP + COOK TIME 10 MINUTES
MAKES 3 CUPS

1 (25-ounce) bottle extra-virgin olive oil
2 tablespoons salt
¼ cup minced garlic
1 cup chopped fresh herbs (basil, rosemary, parsley, oregano)

Combine all the ingredients and blend with a blender stick or in a blender until smooth. Transfer to a jar, seal, and store in the fridge for up to 6 months.

MAC NUT
Vinaigrette

Great on salads, as a stir-fry sauce, on rice, or on rice noodles. This sauce is versatile and so good on its own. It will be the star of whatever you pair it with. This sauce is so well balanced with creaminess, sweetness, and acidity.

SERVES 3½ CUPS
PREP TIME 10 MINUTES

3 cups macadamia nuts
1½ cups rice vinegar
¾ cup pure maple syrup
½ cup tamari
¼ cup sesame oil

Place all the ingredients in a blender, and blend on high until the sauce is dreamy and creamy and emulsified. Store in an airtight container in the fridge for up to 1 month.

x **GF**
x **SF**

x **NF**

PANIOLO
Ranch Dressing

One of my favorite snacks in high school was French bread dipped in ranch. When I went vegan, I missed ranch, and store-bought vegan ranch did not satisfy my craving. So I went to work, and this is what I came up with. I still love it after all these years. If you want to make it healthier, you could substitute soaked cashews and water for the vegan mayo.

SERVES 2½ CUPS **PREP TIME** 10 MINUTES

2 cups vegan mayo
½ cup non-dairy milk
1 teaspoon salt
1 teaspoon garlic powder
1 bunch fresh dill, stemmed
  and finely chopped,
    or 2 tablespoons
    dried dill

Combine the vegan mayo, milk, salt, and garlic powder in a blender. Blend until everything is fluid. Add more milk if you like it runnier. With the blender running on low speed, slowly add the dill and continue processing just until the dill is fully incorporated. If you blend in the dill at a higher speed or for too long, the dressing will turn green and will not look like ranch. Store in an airtight container in the fridge for up to 1 month.

x **GF**
x **SF (if you use soy-free vegan mayo)**
x **NF**

Sea Salt

Vinaigrette

Macadamia

Peanut

Ranch

Jar your dressings and never
buy store bought ever again

CASHEW
Caesar Dressing

We should all be able to enjoy a Caesar salad—so because the dressing usually isn't dairy-free and therefore doesn't fit in my vegan diet, I decided to make my own! This is so creamy and savory that you could get away with using it as a dip.

MAKES 2 CUPS **PREP TIME** 10 MINUTES

1 cup cashews
1 cup water
Juice of 1 lemon
½ large sushi-size
   seaweed sheet
¼ cup tamari

x GF
x SF
x NF

Mix all the ingredients together in a blender, and process for 30 seconds. You can thin it out by adding more water and tamari. If you desire it thicker add more cashews. Transfer to an airtight container and keep in the fridge for up to 3 days.

Recipe Notes:
Some people soak their cashews for an hour or even overnight before using in recipes like this one. Soaking is not necessary, though, if you are in a rush—especially if you have a high-speed blender.

BOMB-DIGGITY
Peanut Dressing

This dressing is the bomb. It's good on everything! On a salad, in a stir fry, on rice, and even in a tortilla. At the café, we used to serve it with our summer rolls. A lot of times, I think the rolls are just a vessel for the sauce.

MAKES 2½ CUPS **PREP TIME** 15 MINUTES

1 jar (16 ounces) smooth peanut butter

2 tablespoons grated fresh ginger

2 tablespoons minced garlic

1½ teaspoons salt

2 tablespoons chopped fresh cilantro

½ teaspoon curry powder

½ teaspoon red pepper flakes

1 ½ cups rice vinegar

1 cup water

1 cup sugar

Mix all the ingredients in a blender, and process on medium speed until and the sauce is smooth and pourable. Store in an airtight container in the fridge for up to 1 month.

Recipe Notes:
You can sub almond butter for peanut butter and maple syrup for sugar if you want a slightly healthier sauce.

x GF

x SF

x NF

HAWAIIAN ISLAND
Dressing

This is my take on the classic Thousand Island dressing. It's especially delicious on our Taco Salad (page 117), but it is also tasty on burgers, tacos, and so much more. Get creative.

MAKES 2½ CUPS **PREP TIME** 10 MINUTES

2 cups vegan mayo

1 teaspoon rice vinegar

1 cup ketchup

2 tablespoons relish

In a blender, combine the vegan mayo, vinegar, and ketchup. Blend until smooth, transfer to a bowl, and stir in the relish. Store in an airtight container in the fridge for up to a month.

x **GF**

x **SF (if you use soy-free vegan mayo)**

x **NF**

SIMPLE
Dressing

Don't let the name fool you—although this dressing is simple to make, the flavor is big and bold. If I'm looking for a light dressing, I sub rice vinegar. When I want a heavier dressing, I use balsamic.

MAKES ¾ CUPS **PREP TIME** 5 MINUTES

½ **cup extra-virgin olive oil**
¼ **cup rice vinegar or**
   balsamic vinegar
2 **teaspoons pure maple syrup**
½ **teaspoon salt**
⅛ **teaspoon freshly ground**
   black pepper

Combine all the ingredients in a Mason jar, and shake well. Seal the jar and store it on the counter for up to 1 month.

x **GF**
x **SF**
x **NF**

CASHEW

Cheese

This can be used as the base for many recipes: lasagna, mac and cheese, enchilada pie, soup and dressings, filler for spanakopita, and so much more. See what you can dream up!

MAKES 2½ CUPS **PREP TIME** 5 MINUTES

2 cups cashews

1½ to 2 cups water (depending on the consistency you are looking for. Start with less, then add in more as needed.)

3 tablespoons tamari

Combine all the ingredients in a blender, and begin processing on low speed, then gradually increase the speed to high; blend until smooth. Transfer to an airtight container and store in the fridge for up to two days.

Recipe Notes:

For a cream-based dessert, sub sugar/or syrup for the tamari. This is great for filling pastries!

x **GF**

x **SF (if you sub 1½ teaspoons salt for the tamari)**

NO BBQ NEEDED
Sauce

Do you know anyone who doesn't like BBQ sauce? I can't think of anyone. It is as American as ketchup. There are so many good jarred varieties, but you will have no need for them when you see how easy it is to make. I enjoy it on cauliflower (page 163), on a baked potato, or slathered on a veggie burger. So grab your ingredients and give it a whirl.

MAKES 2 CUPS **PREP TIME** 5 MINUTES

1 cup ketchup
2 tablespoons pure maple syrup
1 teaspoon rice vinegar or apple cider vinegar
1 teaspoon dark chili powder
2 tablespoons olive oil
3 tablespoons water
Pinch of salt

Combine all the ingredients in a blender. Start processing on low, then gradually bring it up to high until all the ingredients are blended together. Use right away or store in a mason jar in the fridge for up to 2 months.

CHIPOTLE
Cream

Great for tacos, nachos, as a dip, a topping on chili, or as a dressing on taco salad, this sauce adds a kick to anything.

MAKES 1 CUPS **PREP TIME** 5 MINUTES

1 container (8 ounces) vegan
   sour cream
2 whole chipotle chilies
   in adobo sauce (from a
   4-ounce can)

Combine the sour cream and chipotles in a blender, and process until smooth. Transfer to an airtight container and keep in the fridge for up to a week.

x GF
x SF (if you use soy-free vegan
sour cream)
x NF

YUMS
+ TREATS
Naughty but nice

MANGO
Nice Cream

Better than ice cream, and nice to your body. This was a favorite at the café and loved by all. Eating mangoes is known to prevent cancer, lower cholesterol, help clear skin pores, improve eye health, and boost your immune system, among other great benefits.

MAKES 1 ½ PINTS **PREP TIME** 5 MINUTES **CHURN TIME** 30 MINUTES

2 (13.5-ounce) cans coconut milk, chilled

¾ cup sugar

1½ cups fresh or frozen diced mango

Combine all the ingredients in a blender, and process until the mango is puréed into the milk. Pour into an ice cream maker, and follow the instructions provided on the machine. You can also enjoy this as a milk shake right from the blender.

Recipe Notes:
- Make sure your milk and ice cream machine are cold to make it easier to spin.
- You can use the coconut milk and sugar as a base for any ice cream flavor you want to make: cocoa powder, peanut butter, mint chocolate chip, and on and on.

x GF
x SF
x NF

Recipe Notes:

- Lilikoi seeds have different supplements that you do not get from most fruits, so they should be eaten with the lilikoi! Don't be afraid to eat them. Your heart and intestines will truly thank you.

- The long list of health benefits commonly attributed to lilikoi is due to the nutrient, mineral, and vitamin content of the fruit, which includes antioxidants, flavonoids, vitamin A, vitamin C, riboflavin, niacin, iron, magnesium, phosphorus, potassium, copper, fiber, and protein

SWEET AND SOUR

Lilikoi Cake

SERVVES 8 SLICES
TOTAL PREP TIME 45 MINUTES

Lilikoi means passion fruit in Hawaiian. It is sweet and sour. It was the flavor behind the original Hawaiian punch. It has this beautiful yellow or orange flesh and lots of seeds. The seeds have so many nutrients, so I decided to grind them with the pulp in our blender and make a cake. In Hawaii, lilikoi are ripe for the picking six months out of the year, and we were so lucky to have our own vine on the fence at the restaurant. You can find them at specialty stores on the mainland, or plant a vine of your own.

For the cake:

About 15 lilikoi (passion fruit), blended whole with seeds (You'll have 1½ cups of purée; set aside ¼ cup for the icing)

1½ cups water

½ cup olive oil, plus more for oiling the pan

3 cups flour, plus more for brushing the pan

2 cups sugar

2 teaspoons baking soda

1 teaspoon salt

For the icing:

2 cups powdered sugar

¼ cup reserved lilikoi purée

x **GF (if you replace flour with 3 cups oat flour and use oat flour to flour pan)**

x **SF**

x **NF**

To make the cake: Preheat the oven to 375°F. Oil and flour a Bundt pan.

In a medium bowl, combine 1¼ cups of the puréed lilikoi, the water, and the olive oil. In a large bowl, mix together the flour, sugar, baking soda, and salt. Slowly add the wet ingredients to the flour mixture; mix until blended. Pour the batter into the prepared pan, and bake for 30 to 40 minutes, until you can poke it with a toothpick in center and it comes out clean. Remove from the oven and let the cake cool for about 30 minutes before icing.

To make the icing: In a medium bowl, whisk the powdered sugar and ¼ cup reserved lilikoi purée until smooth. When the cake is no longer warm to the touch, invert it onto a platter, and pour the icing over top. You will want to thank me for this one, so you are welcome!

G TO THE
Free Brownies

Ooey, gooey, chocolatey, and chewy. These are just as good if not better than regular brownies. They may be free of gluten, wheat, soy, dairy, and eggs, but they're full of flavor and love! Do not ask why, just try them and you will never doubt me again. This is indulgence at its finest!

MAKES 9 LARGE BROWNIES **TOTAL PREP TIME** 10 MINUTES

Cooking spray
2 cups brown rice flour
2 cups sugar
1 cup cocoa powder
2 teaspoon baking powder
1½ teaspoons xanthan gum
1 teaspoon baking soda
1 teaspoon salt
½ cup olive oil
1½ cups water
½ cup vegan chocolate chips

Preheat the oven to 350°F. Line a 9 x 9-inch baking dish with parchment, and grease the parchment with coconut oil or olive oil cooking spray.

In a large bowl, mix together the flour, sugar, cocoa powder, baking powder, xanthan gum, baking soda, and salt, and then slowly stir in the water and oil. Mix until blended. Pour the batter into the prepared pan. Sprinkle with the chocolate chips, and bake for 40 minutes or until you can poke the center with a toothpick and it comes out clean.

Remove from the oven and let cool for about 30 minutes, then remove from the pan. Cut into 9 pieces. I love to serve them warm with vegan ice cream melting on top. Pure G to the Free indulgence!

x **GF**
x **SF**
x **NF**

NOT YOUR MAMA'S
Chocolate Chip Cookies

I don't know when my love affair with cookies started, but it's been a long romance that seems to only grow stronger. When I started changing my diet, I realized how many of my treats did not honor my body. That is when I started working on this recipe. It eats like a cookie but in its healthiest form. It is both vegan and gluten-free, but no one will ever know!

SERVES 48 SMALL COOKIES **TOTAL PREP TIME** 35 MINUTES

1 cup shortening or vegan butter

1½ cups organic granulated sugar

1½ cups organic brown sugar

1 (12-ounce) package organic silken firm tofu

4½ cups brown rice flour

2 teaspoons baking soda

1 teaspoon salt

1 teaspoon xanthan gum

2 cups vegan chocolate chips

Preheat the oven to 350°F. Line a baking sheet with parchment.

In a mixer or bowl, combine the palm fruit oil, tofu, granulated sugar, and brown sugar. Paddle or beat until light and fluffy. Add the tofu, flour, baking soda, salt, and xanthan gum, and mix until everything is incorporated. Fold in the chocolate chips.

Use a spoon or ice cream scoop to portion the dough onto the prepared baking sheet. Bake for 10 to 12 minutes, depending on how you like them, soft or crunchy.

x **SF**
x **NF**

SWEET + STICKY
Rice Cereal Treats

Is it even possible to not love rice cereal treats? They are light, crispy, and always a crowd pleaser. This recipe requires no baking, so it makes them easy to make on the fly. There are so many different vegan marshmallows and organic rice cereals these days. It really is easier than ever to make vegan rice cereal treats.

MAKES 12 GIANT TREATS **TOTAL PREP TIME** 15 MINUTES

4 tablespoons vegan butter
2 (10-ounce) packages vegan marshmallows
1 box (8½ cups) organic rice cereal

x **GF**
x **SF**
x **NF**

Line a 9 x 13-inch baking pan with parchment. Have plastic wrap or gloves nearby.

Melt the butter in large, heavy stockpot over medium heat. Reduce the heat to medium low, add the vegan marshmallows, and stir. Keep the heat low so the marshmallows melt rather than burn. Once almost all the marshmallows have melted, add the rice cereal, and stir. Transfer to the prepared pan and use plastic wrap or gloves to press the treats down with your hands. You want to make the treats condensed and solid so they stay together. Let the treat cool down, then cut into 12 squares and enjoy. Leftover treats will keep in an airtight container on the counter for up to five days.

Recipe Notes:

- Use this recipe as a base for other raw fruit pies. Swap out macadamia nuts for other nuts. For a Hawaiian-style pie, use banana and mango instead of apple. I always say with everything in life, do not put limits on what you can create!
- Apple helps keep so many parts and functions of the body healthy; it really is true that an apple a day keeps the doc away!

ALOHA *Apple Pie*

SERVES 8 **TOTAL PREP TIME** 35 MINUTES

It is no secret that I love my yums. I mean, I chose to go to pastry school because of my love of all things sweet. There are times where my love of sugar does not serve my vessel, and I must find ways to satisfy my cravings that are not a negative for my body. In walks this raw apple pie. It does the job of many, as it is great for breakfast, a snack, or to replace the traditional baked dessert. I find a food processor works best for this recipe. You can assemble it in a pie plate or spring form pan, or you can also make mini mason jar pies.

2 cups macadamia nuts

4 pitted dates (I get the ones rolled in coconut)

6 apples (I like sweet ones like Gala or Fuji), skin on, cored and cut into chunks

1 teaspoon ground cinnamon

Pinch of salt

Squeeze of fresh lemon juice

x **SF**

x **GF**

Put the macadamia nuts and 2 of the dates in a food processor; process until the oil starts to release from the nuts and the dates start to form a dough.

If using a spring form pan, line it with parchment. (No need to use parchment if using a pie dish or mason jars.) Transfer the crust to the pan or dish(es), and push with your hands to evenly spread out the dough. It should cover the bottom and about ¼ inch up the sides. Set aside.

Without cleaning the processor, add 2 more dates and a squeeze of lemon, and process for 20 seconds to break the dates into small pieces. Set aside in a large.

Use the food processor's grater attachment to finely chop your apples. Add the chopped apples to the bowl with the date-lemon mixture, and toss well. Taste it. Is it sweet enough? If not, add more sweetener; I sometimes add a little maple syrup. Once it is to your liking, transfer the apple mix to your pie crust. I push down with parchment paper to get it flat and uniform.

No need to bake! Top it with berries and a little coconut cream (the thick layer in the can). Refrigerate until ready to serve.

SWEET-CHEAT
Cookie Dough Treats

I believe you should have a small cheat with every diet. This is my cheat food whenever I am cleansing. It hits my sweet spot but never gives me a sugar rush. I love cookie dough, so I enjoy these raw. They are also delicious baked. It's up to you!

MAKES 8 COOKIES **TOTAL PREP TIME** 5 MINUTES

½ cup peanut butter or
   almond butter
1 cup almond flour
¼ to ⅓ cup pure maple syrup
½ cup stevia-sweetened
   chocolate chips

In a mixing bowl, stir together the peanut butter and almond flour, then add the maple syrup and mix well (it should resemble cookie dough). Fold in the chocolate chips. Store the dough in an airtight container in the fridge for up to a week. Beware when it's cold, as it is a bit harder to scoop.

Recipe Notes:

To bake these as cookies, just preheat the oven to 350°F, scoop spoonfuls onto a parchment-lined baking sheet, and bake for 11 minutes.

x GF
x SF

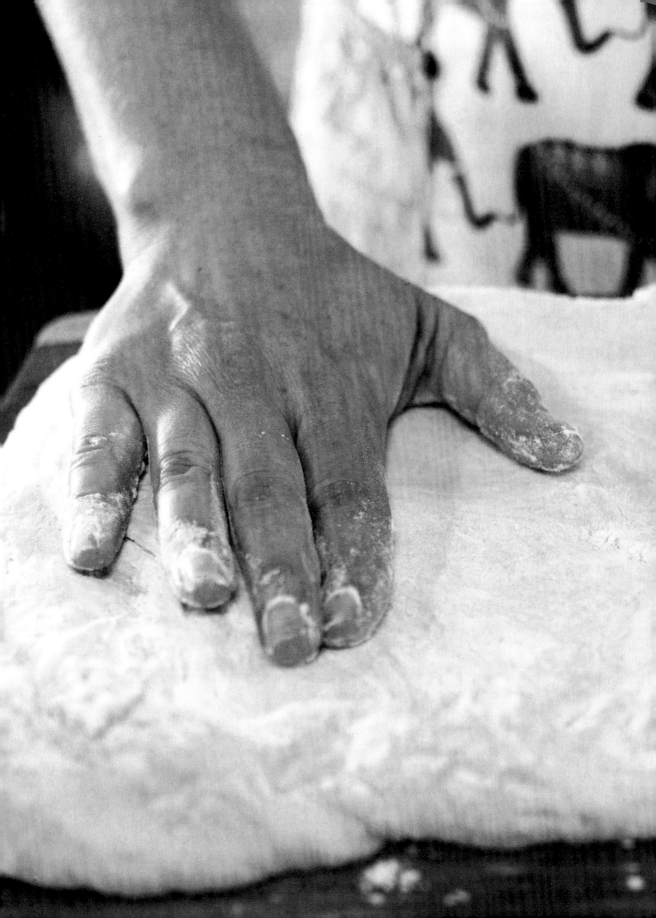

the greatest tool in the kitchen

IS YOUR OWN HANDS

EASY LIKE SUNDAY MORNING
Cinnamon Rolls

MAKES 12 **TOTAL PREP TIME** 1½ HOURS

If there is anything better than the delightful smell of freshly baked cinnamon rolls, it would have to be the ooey, gooey sweet taste! The original recipe is full of fat, depleted flour, and eggs, so I came up with a recipe that retained the flavor we all know and love without the junk stuff. You can make the dough days ahead and store it, or you can use it right away. I top mine with a coconut royal icing. When I serve these, everyone agrees . . . it is not enough to eat just one. You can double the recipe and make Texas-size rolls, as well. Maybe not easy, but perfect on Sunday morning!

6 cups spelt flour

¾ cup sugar, divided

2 packets (¼ ounce) of active yeast (4½ teaspoons)

1 cup very warm water

½ cup vegan butter, melted

1 teaspoon salt

1 cup almond milk

2 teaspoons ground cinnamon

1½ cups powdered sugar

1 to 1½ tablespoons coconut milk or water

Preheat the oven to 350°F. Grease a 9-inch pie plate or square baking dish.

In the bowl of an electric mixer, combine the flour and ¼ cup of the sugar; set aside. In a measuring cup or bowl, mix together the yeast, ¼ cup of the sugar, and the warm water. Let stand for 10 minutes until foamy, and then pour into the bowl with the flour mixture, along with ¼ cup of the melted butter. Mix until a soft dough forms. Scrape the dough into a lightly floured bowl, cover with plastic wrap, and let rise for 30 minutes, it should double in size.

When the dough is finished rising, scrape it onto a floured surface and roll it into a rectangle about 9 x 13. Brush the remaining ¼ cup of melted butter over the top, sprinkle with the remaining ¼ cup of sugar, and dust with the cinnamon.

Next, starting at one short end, begin to roll up the dough tightly (see photos).

Pinch it together at the seam so it does not roll back open. With a sharp or serrated knife, cut the log into 12 rolls. I start in the middle and cut three on each side, then I cut those into two.

Arrange the rolls in the pie plate and bake for 20 to 30 minutes or until lightly golden brown. Remove from the oven to cool.

Meanwhile, combine the powdered sugar and coconut milk in a blender, and process until smooth. Arrange the rolls on individual plates, and drizzle the blended frosting on top.

x GF (if you replace the flour with brown rice flour and 3 teaspoons of xanthan gum)
x SF (if you use soy-free vegan butter)
x NF (if you replace the almond milk with hemp, coconut, oat, or seed milk)

CUCKOO FOR COCOA
Pudding Cups

You will be the star of any age group with this dessert. From a small kids' party to a large wedding, it is a crowd pleaser! Make sure you are equipped with long-handled spoons—or you will have sticky hands.

SERVES 8 (EITHER AS A PIE OR AS INDIVIDUAL CUPS)
TOTAL PREP TIME 10 MINUTES

**2 cans (13.5 ounce)
   coconut milk**
1½ cups sugar
¾ cup cocoa
8 tablespoons cornstarch
2 cans of water

Pour the coconut milk into a medium saucepan, then fill one of the cans with water and add that, too, followed by the sugar and cocoa powder. Place the pan over medium heat and cook, stirring frequently, until bubbly, about 10 minutes. Pour one can-full of water into a small bowl, add the cornstarch, and whisk with a fork until smooth. Add this to the hot coconut milk mixture, let it cook until it's bubbly and thick, about 2 minutes, and then remove the pan from the heat.

Pour the hot mixture into tall Mason jars, and let cool slightly before serving, or refrigerate and serve chilled. You can also pour it into a precooked pie crust and refrigerate overnight before slicing and serving. For an extra-special treat, top it with coconut whipped cream. The cups or pie will last for up to 1 week in the fridge.

x **GF**
x **SF**
x **NF**

TAKE ME TO THAILAND:

Mango Sticky Rice

This is one of my favorite desserts in the world. I always order it when I am out for Thai food. I wanted to learn how to make it so I could enjoy it at home. You can use any rice, but sweet rice is the best.

SERVES 6 **TOTAL PREP TIME** 35 MINUTES

1½ **cups sweet rice**

2 **cups water**

1½ **cups full fat coconut milk**

¾ **cup sugar**

2 **mangoes, peeled and sliced**

x **GF**

x **SF**

x **NF**

Combine the rice and water in a saucepan, and bring to a boil. Cover, reduce the heat to low, and simmer for 30 minutes or until all the water is absorbed.

Combine the coconut milk and sugar in a small saucepan over medium heat, and stir for a few minutes until the sugar is completely dissolved into the milk.

Pour the warm milk over the rice, and stir. Remove the pan from the heat and scoop the rice into bowls or individual plates. Top with the sliced mango (or your favorite fruit), and enjoy!

Recipe Notes:

I also love topping my sticky rice with papaya when mango is out of season. Goji berries or any dried fruit can be a fun variation, as well.

PROVIDE FOR YOUR TRIBE

Connections are everything

Living in Hawaii

Living in Hawaii, I have the privilege of being in a place that focuses on a more relaxed lifestyle. We call it Hawaii time. Never be in too much of a hurry, and embody the aloha spirit. It naturally slows you down. It makes you aware of what energy you carry. You are known here more for who you are than what you do or have in your bank account. Value is placed on being a steward to the land and the people. Kauai, the island I live on, is small, you want to make sure you are kind to everyone because more often than not you are connected to them through work, family, or mutual friends. The island makes it easy to lead with your heart. The island has also taught me that what we do individually affects the whole.

Living on an island, that has 2500 miles of vast ocean between us and any other major land mass makes it easy to see that the way we currently live isn't sustainable. It is like a microcosm of our planet. We ship most things in and have to ship our recycling out. At times swimming in the pristine waters, you see the plastic bits floating by you. After a large swell, our beaches are littered with plastic. It doesn't end there. From all our land-based refuse, you can actually see how big our landfill grows and grows. You can see the impact our consumption has on this beautiful island. If you litter or don't recycle, you will physically see it.

I always prefer simple flowers
in reusable glasses or jars.

MADE WITH LOVE –
– X X X X –

Vegan and More

Being vegan means so much more to me than what I put on my plate. I do my best to walk my talk. I care so deeply about the future of health, my children, my future grandchildren, and the planet. When I started transitioning my diet, I began to see how wasteful I had been and how our society is programmed for waste: paper plates, plastic plates, chemicals in the cleaners we bring into our homes, plastic bags in our lunches, and Styrofoam containers. It only takes a little research to see that we can do better. So that's what I did. I started making small changes in my life. I stopped using paper and plastic plates in my home and parties. I began supporting restaurants that use biodegradable take out. I pack my own water bottle, and if I must splurge I buy glass and reuse it. Over the years, I have started a small collection of party boxes where I always have enough to entertain with, without going to the party store. I bought fabric I loved in yards and cut into streamer size strips, and I use these to decorate my house for the kids' birthday. There are so many little things you can do that will make a significant impact.

I just want you to start. Remember every journey begins with a first step. Start exploring how you can reduce, reuse and recycle in your life. Once I started, I personally began to see how things were made and if they didn't support my health, or the planet's health, I would find a replacement that did or go without.

Beyond the Plate

My current lifestyle reflects compassion and a drive to do better in all areas of my life. What does that look like? I do not purchase fabrics, leather, or anything that comes from an animal. I know this may seem daunting at first. There are so many replacements available these days, so instead of feeling deprived, see that it opens you up to all new brands and styles.

When you go to the store opt for the organic or more natural brand of what you usually use. There are replacements for almost everything you use, that is comparable in quality. Without the chemicals that aren't good for your body or the planet.

When it comes to beauty products, I only use organic, pure, natural products, and make sure they are not tested on animals. Conventional beauty products contain chemicals, and many of them are cancer causing. This is something many of you use every day, and our skin literally eats it. Look at the ingredients on the package. Be thoughtful and think, is this something you feel ok with, knowing that your body will be processing it every day, the same goes for

makeup. Look for products that use only natural dyes and ingredients. When I made the switch, my skin became luminous and healthier. Remember, all the products we use, return to the earth when they go down the drain or to the landfill.

Entertaining is so fun, but as a party planner, I can tell you, it is wasteful. I see it at parties all the time: paper plates and cups, napkins, plastic straws, containers, and more. I see it in restaurants. I sadly see it everywhere. We have become a disposable society. We don't have to be. As you will see in the photos, there are so many ways to make a table or party charming without spending any money, besides your initial investment.

When I clean, I use natural cleaners. When we don't use natural soaps and the like, we unsuspectingly bring poisons into our homes. Although the products work and everything may look clean, they are leaving a layer of poison on everything in your home. Instead, switch to natural cleaners and see if you can breathe better in your home.

Switch out your detergent to one that is natural and biodegradable. Our skin breathes in the soap we wear and sleep in. Scents are okay, just make sure it comes from an essential oil and is not chemical based. New research is showing that the synthetic fragrances we have in all our products are making us sick.

When I made the switch, I felt so much better. Over time my family's allergy symptoms disappeared. If you can invest in cleaning bottles you can refill yourself it makes a big difference. There are so many essential oils that can be mixed with water that do an incredible job. I believe that you want to use products that you would be okay consuming internally – because everything we use to clean we consume, either by touching, eating, or absorbing through your skin.

I make my kids lunches every day for school. I am amazed when I go to their school how many single-use products I see! Packaging galore but there are ways to avoid it. Changing from Ziploc bags to reusable or paper bags is a good option. I use small Pyrex dishes as containers, and we have never had one break. Use BPA (bisphenol-A)-free plastic containers. Find lunchboxes that hold food and keep it cold. Thermoses are amazing for soups and smoothies alike.

I always try to use real glasses and plates when entertaining. Not only does it make the event more special, it also is better for the Earth.

MADE WITH LOVE
– XXXX –

Always try to keep traditions in the family, but healthier.

Living in Hawaii

Outside the Home

When you eat out, patronize and support restaurants that have biodegradable to-go containers. Say no to Styrofoam! This way you know that the containers you use won't still be around when your great, great, grandkids are around. Try to go without a straw. BYOS! (bring your own straw), there are so many great reusable straws on the market-glass, stainless steel, and so many more. If the restaurant doesn't have biodegradable straws, go without the straw. If you have time, you can always dine at home and make a meal with the recipes in this book!

If we open our eyes, we can see the overwhelming waste in our society. There are so many problems we can focus our energy on. Since changing my lifestyle, I can tell you, making little changes can add up. In the last 11 years, my footprint on this earth is so much smaller than it's ever been. A lot of times we feel like we have no power to make changes, but every day we vote by choosing what we put our money toward. I have decided to put my

money and energy toward companies that care about my health my family's health and the health of the planet. This is my rule, and there have been very few exceptions since I put it in place. The best part about this is my kids are being raised with this knowledge, and this will be their norm—taking care of their bodies and our planet.

FROM WASTE TO CHANGE

The best way to change the world is with small manageable steps. What small steps can you take now to change your habits for the better? What can you do today to feel like you are part of the solution and not the problem?

Through all the problems we face, I love hearing solutions. I invite you to stay in touch with me through email or social media and let me know what you do or what changes you have made.

Love Hollan

CHOOSE

your
TRIBE

The best way to change the world
is with small manageable steps.
What small steps can you take now
to change your habits for the better?
What can you do today to feel like
you are part of the solution and
not the problem?

COOKS
JOURNAL

Notes, notes, notes

Notes

Cooking is a practical art – the more you do it, the better you get. Give yourself time if you are new to the kitchen or ingredients. It took me time to create these recipes and perfect them, and it will take time for you to make it to your taste buds.

I consider fruits and veggies free foods. I don't think I can overdo them. I have never said, "I'm so overfilled from that salad" or, "I shouldn't have had another apple."

Eating vegan opened me up to a whole new way of eating plant-based foods.

So, I added more to my diet. If in a hurry, it's easy to throw together meals if you keep your pantry and fridge stocked up.

If you are stressed for time, give yourself an hour to prep ingredients so you can make them quickly on weekdays.

TIPS

- Put on your favorite music while you cook, it sets the mood.

- I wear aprons because they are cute, not to protect my clothes. It is like an accessory.

- Don't let chefs complicate food too much for you. Delicious eating can be simple.

- Eating vegan is one of the best things you can do for the planet, Every meal helps.

- Ask yourself regularly: what are three things you are grateful for in this moment?

- Water is the most cleansing substance we have, drink accordingly.

- Our thoughts feed our soul.

- I have lived without a microwave for 15 years, and I'm proof it's possible.

Pesticides are all over our food. I try to buy organic any chance I get. Shop accordingly.

DIRTY DOZEN AND THE CLEAN FIFTEEN

Take a look at the following list (right) and try to buy at least the dirty dozen as organic.

THE CLEAN FIFTEEN

Avocado

Sweet corn – (non-GMO)

Pineapple

Cabbage

Sweet peas – frozen

Onions

Asparagus

Mangoes

Papayas

Kiwi

Eggplant

Honeydew melon

Grapefruit

Cantaloupe

Cauliflower

THE DIRTY DOZEN

Strawberries

Apples

Nectarines – imported

Peaches

Celery

Grapes

Cherries

Spinach

Tomatoes

Sweet bell peppers

Cherry tomatoes

Cucumbers

Tools of the Trade

There are so many ways you can make these recipes without my fancy tools. Listed below is the equipment I used in the writing of this cookbook and a few appliance brands I recommend and have in my kitchen.

ELECTRICAL APPLIANCES

Blender— Vitamix is the best of the best in my opinion

Food processor—I love my Cuisinart (ranging from 2 to 11 cups)

Mixer—Kitchen-aid mixer is my favorite

Juicer—I have a Greenstar, a Champion, and a Breville. (Brevilles easy clean-up makes it my fave)

Blender stick—I love Cuisinart Blender stick

Cold Brew Coffee Tower—YAMA

Ice cream maker

EVERYDAY ITEMS

Cutting board

Sauté steel pans, stainless steel various sizes

Cupcake pan

Half sheet pan (cookie sheet)

Parchment paper

Glass tupperware

Loaf pan

Waffle iron

Bundt pan

Can opener

Yama cold brew

UTENSILS

Mixing bowls

Measuring cups

Measuring spoons

Mixing spoons

Spatula

Whisk

Tongs

Masher

Skillet

Griddle

Large bowl

Mason jars

Jars of all sizes

Metal straw

Matcha tea set

A good knife—I love Wustof and Shun

Strainer

Nut milk Strainer

Pitcher

Ice cream scoop 2 oz and 4 oz.

COOKING ITEMS

Large boiling pot

Spring Form pan

Pie pan

Pots and Pans

You can use any brand for ingredients in the recipe.
That being said find what products work for you.

A few brands I love are...

International Harvest is my one stop source for all certified organic dried foods, nuts, trail mixes, granolas and other special super foods.

Veganaise for vegan mayo

Daiya for vegan cheese

Lighthouse Fakin Bakin for bacon

Tambor for açai

And the rest is up to you.

Kalia and Sadie in New York, we were always walking from vegan café to vegan café

traveling memories

I love traveling so much. When you get out of your everyday life and have time to think, it is amazing how much you learn, about food, life, other cultures and yourself

Cruising the Malecon, Havana Cuba

From Kauai to New York, I travel the United States and globally to find inspiration everywhere I go.

FOOD

feeds your body

GRATITUDE

feeds your

SOUL

CAFFE COCO

CAFFE COCO

OPEN

BAKE MY DAY

Various old snaps of the Cafe and signage, such a wonderful life and creative cafe.

This is the café right before I sold it.

MANTRA

eat healthy everyday

Index

Index

Index

Index

Index

MADE WITH LOVE
- xxxx -

Thanks

Creating a cookbook, takes a village: a village of people who have skills—from organization to design to photography. It took many talented people who had the passion and experience in areas where I did not. I just had a dream of sharing my recipes. You all are responsible for me living it.

To Haleem, thank you for your unconditional support for all my crazy undertakings. You push me to be better and go farther than I do myself.

To my three children, Jaden, Kalia, and Lilah, this is for you. I love you dearly, and thank you for encouraging me to follow my passion. I want to be a better person because of all of you. If this book becomes nothing more than a cookbook on your shelves, I will die happy knowing you get to share my recipes with your children and their children and so on.

To Pop and Lulu, for always guiding me to follow my heart and always supporting my endeavors. You teach me by example of never being stuck in one vision, job, or dream.

To my mama in heaven, for loving me enough to believe in myself.

To Tonimom, for being my Earth Mama and always grounding me and accepting me however I am.

To Anthony J.W. Benson, my creative partner and publisher, for your remarkable vision, expertise, and guidance on not only how to write a cookbook, but also how to give birth to it with integrity, beauty and authenticity.

To Elliot, for believing in me and always showing up. You are so talented in so many ways—design, websites, photography, video, and so much more. Thank you for sharing your endless talents for this book.

To Sadie, thank you for showing up for all the crazy fun shoots and edits. You are my best student. And it's true what they say: the student eventually becomes the teacher.

To Chris, Lei, and Jayda, thank you for all you have taught me, all the help you have given, and for so many laughs. "Hold on Ellen, Oprah's calling."

To Tessa, my dearest, thank you for being my therapist and sounding board. I love you and your family (Blaise and Monet) so much. Friends are the family you choose. I chose wisely.

To Alicia and team, thanks for your undying support and helpful contributions.

To Shana, for all the love and edits.

To Gayna, CharLee, Sheridan, Heather and Peggy for helping to bring the words, images, and beauty cohesively together.

Lewis Howes, my angel, thank you for believing I could push past mediocrity and strive for greatness. This book is that first step.

To Chris Lee, for giving me a new lease on life and allowing me space and safety to bloom.

To Bryce, for the beautiful photos of my food and Hawaii scattered throughout the cookbook. I want to see the world the way you do through a lens.

To Meg, for seeing something special in me and helping me take the first leap toward dreamlife 2.0.

To Lorrie & Neil, you are angels. I have so much gratitude for your belief in me to make this book a reality. Luna and Skye, I will make you cookies for life.

To everyone at Eat Healthy, Caffe Coco, and Hippie Café, thank you for your part in my life. I am a sum of all my parts and can be no stronger than my team, so thank you for being on the team.

Minds, Dave, Halia, Lea, and Hunter, you have given me family on Kauai. How can I ever repay you?

To all my friends, I love you, and you have encouraged me every step of the way.

To Blenda, Raymond, Mateo, and Santi. I love you all. Blenda, your talent with a camera amazes me. How lucky am I that one of my best friends shot the cover and so many photos in this book. I owe you so many meals.

To Tom and Andi, serendipitous how we met, but it was meant to be. Thank you for the beautiful photos and the best company. See you in Austria.

To my family, my brothers David, Sam, Brent, and Pete, and my sister Aisha, and my cousins Sammy and Rosie, growing up with all of you literally shaped my life. There is no one I would rather do it with. To all your families, Jules, Chrissy, Erica, David, Gracie, Mia, and Quinn, I love you. Rainer, thank you for always being there for me.

Thank you, Kub, for the edit and for the unconditional encouragement.

Thank you to Diana for always being my cheerleader.

Thank you to Alana, my Kauai vegan sister, for the beautiful and thoughtful forward. I will cook with you in the kitchen anytime!

Thank you to John and PJ, who are the new owners of Eat Healthy.

Thank you to all the organic farmers on the planet. You are the stewards of Mother Earth, her precious land, and all our health.

And thank you, TO YOU, for reading this, and to all small business owners that carry this book at their store. I LOVE YOU ALL!

Wishing you vibrant health, *Hollan*

FOR THE READER

Deeper Well Publishing is as a unique boutique publishing and multimedia company designed to assist seekers of all backgrounds and beliefs in expanding their minds and exploring the depths of health, consciousness, and spirituality. Through our books and products, we endeavor to help you deepen your quest for knowledge, and enhance your quality of life. We welcome you to dive in and explore the deeper well with us.

FOR THE WRITER

Do you desire to discover your inner-writer, but also clarify your purpose, invigorate your spirit, and be inspired to express your individuality?

Do you wish to share your writing with the world, for all to read?

Deeper Well Publishing, and it's unique author services, were created, so you don't have to take the journey alone. We offer a one-on-one safe-haven for fellow writers to refine their work, gain feedback, insight, inspiration, guidance, tips, tools, encouragement, and much more. If you want to mine your soul and awaken the quiet giant of creativity that has been lying dormant within you and share your shining writer's soul, then we invite you to explore how we can help you manifest your dream of becoming a published author. Or if you are already a writer, learn how to receive assistance, support, and production of your next project.

DEEPER WELL
PUBLISHING

WRITING · CONSULTING · COACHING · EDITING
DESIGN · PROMOTION · MARKETING · DISTRIBUTION
WAREHOUSING · FULFILLMENT

www.deeperwellpublishing.com

DEEPER WELL PUBLISHING
OFFERS THE BEST IN
CREATIVE BOUTIQUE AUTHOR
SERVICES AND IS EAGER
TO BE OF SERVICE FOR
ALL YOUR WRITING AND
PUBLISHING NEEDS.

When Every Breath
Becomes a Prayer

A Novel

SUSAN PLUNKET

IN RHYTHM
WITH YOUR SOUL

BREAK THROUGH THE BARRIERS TO BEING CREATIVE
FACE YOUR DEMONS AND DANCE

POLLYANNA BLANCO

Foreword by Sharon Young,
3 Time World Professional Exhibition Dance Champion

21 DAY
SUPERSTAR
CLEANSE

- 75+ Nutritious Vegan
  & Plant-based Recipes
- Guilt-Free Indulgence &
  No Calorie Restrictions
- Daily Wellness Advice &
  Inspirational Affirmations
- 20+ Invigorating Yoga
  Poses & Fitness Tips

RAINBEAU MARS

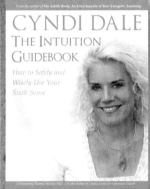

From the author of *The Subtle Body: An Encyclopedia of Your Energetic Anatomy*

CYNDI DALE
THE INTUITION
GUIDEBOOK

*How to Safely and
Wisely Use Your
Sixth Sense*

EASY TO PREPARE VEGAN
HOME-STYLE RECIPES
+ BEACH INSPIRED LIFESTYLE TIPS
FOR THE ENTIRE FAMILY

GOOD FOOD
Gratitude

HOLLAN
HAWAII

Foreword by Alana Blanchard

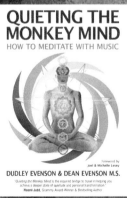

QUIETING THE
MONKEY MIND

HOW TO MEDITATE WITH MUSIC

Foreword by
Joel & Michelle Levey

DUDLEY EVENSON & DEAN EVENSON M.S.

*"Quieting the Monkey Mind is the required bridge to travel in helping you
achieve a deeper state of quietude and personal transformation."*
Naomi Judd, Grammy Award-Winner & Bestselling Author

The Peace Pies Restaurant Recipe Book

FRESH,
Funky, &
RAW!

Delicious & Nutritious
Plant-based,
Gluten-Free,
Soy-Free,
Vegan,
Raw Recipes
to help you
eat healthy
and live well.

JP ALFRED

Foreword by Brigitte Mars, Herbalist and Author of *Rawsome!*

TOGETHERNESS

CYNDI DALE
ANDREW WALD
with Debra Evans

EAT
HEALTHY
everyday

MAHALO

- MADE WITH LOVE -

- X X X X -

NOTES

FAVES

LIVE A HAPPIER, HEALTHIER, AND GREENER LIFE!